15↔51 Secret Regrets *of an*
X-FACTOR
ONLY GOD CAN JUDGE ME NOW

O'GRAM DARCELL

iUniverse

SECRET REGRETS OF AN X-FACTOR
ONLY GOD CAN JUDGE ME NOW

iUniverse books may be ordered through booksellers or by contacting:

iUniverse
1663 Liberty Drive
Bloomington, IN 47403
www.iuniverse.com
1-800-Authors (1-800-288-4677)

ISBN: 978-1-4917-2984-7 (sc)
ISBN: 978-1-4917-3167-3 (e)

Print information available on the last page.

iUniverse rev. date: 04/21/2015

CHAPTER 1

Memories and Events...of my life... from Birth to age Fourteen

(Some Matters mention may have occur after age fourteen)

* Childhood & Family *

Growing up in the household

* My Neighbors & the Neighborhood*

* Friends & Cats*

* My School Days*

Growing Up Into Adulthood

My life began on a day when the world was making big decisions. It was Election Day November 7, 1956 when my mother gave birth to me; oh what a day it was to enter into this world.

I think because I was born on Election Day may be the reason why I never wanted anything to do with any politics; my parents were democrats. Somehow I never became a registered voter or served on anyone's jury duties but that was fine by me!

I'm a strong believer that God Almighty has a plan for each and every one of us; it's up to us to follow that plan according to God's Will. I also believe that everything happens for a reason; even if we don't understand what the reason is for or why.

On the day my mother was in labor with me she was under the effects of a pain medication called Twilight; it had her so high that it caused her to say crazy things during her contractions.

One of the things she yelled out while having a contraction was "get those damn cats out of here". Perhaps she thought she was still at home with all of our cats; this may also explain why I was born with a cat's paw print on my right thigh. I truly believe that my mother somehow marked me with this birthmark.

However, when my father first heard the news that I was born a girl he threw his brand new hat into the Ohio River. My father desperately wanted to have a son; perhaps that's why I grew up being a tomboy trying to do everything a boy could do!

At birth I was named O'Gram Darcell; however, the nurse on duty wanted my middle name to be her first name which was Denise; she took it upon herself and changed my middle name on the hospital birth certificate that has my little footprints on it. Somehow she changed it from Darcell to Denise; therefore the hospital birth certificate and the certificate at the department of vital records has two different middle names listed on them.

My Parents names are Walter and Lena. My father also went under the nickname Jimmy. He wanted my first name to include both Parents names so he came up with the name Jimalena. I never liked O'Gram but I'm glad it wasn't Jimalena!

Speaking of names…Growing up in my household we never referred to each other by our names. My family always called one another by that man, or that woman, or that girl, or that child, or them people; but never calling anyone by their names. # Weird!

I've always been a strong believer that our personalities has something to do with whatever was going on in the universe on the day that we were born; you can say I do believe in Astrology.

I was born under the Zodiac sign Scorpio and as far as what they say about us Scorpios…I can say that I'm a true Scorpio by nature and that's on the real side. # Peep that!

I also believed there could be other forms of life that exist on other planets; I feel that when God created man he didn't just stop there… Come on now…just look at all those planets out there!

However, when I was a little kid, I was terrified of ventriloquist puppets; I used to think that they were some kind of alien creatures that came from another planet…Silly Me.

As far as the little childhood beliefs; I can say that my childhood was pretty much like any other normal child's life. I went out trick-or- treating on Halloween; I also believed in Santa Claus and the Tooth Fairy and I even believed in the Easter bunny.

I loved getting dressed up and going to Church on Easter Sunday and showing off my new outfit. The night before Easter my mother would always fix my hair in Shirley Temple curls and put panties on my head to keep my curls in place. # Imagine that!

My mother only sent me to a hair dresser once in my lifetime and while trying to rinse the shampoo out of my hair; she almost flooded her shop. I never went to another hair dresser since then!

However growing up, my childhood was no walk in the park; I came from a very dysfunctional family. There was always lots of cursing, fussing and fighting all of the time. I guess it's safe to say that alcohol was the reason behind most of the problems!

This may also explain why I'm a night owl and like sleeping during the daytime; all the confusion that was going on in my household made it really impossible to get any sleep at night.

My mother had six children; all girls and no boys! That's something I will always regret not having any brothers to grow up with; # it was just way too much estrogen in my household!

I was born my mother's fifth child next to the baby girl named Vet; my oldest sister's name is Lavon and the three of us all have the same biological father.

People often wonder and ask me how is it possible that the oldest child and the two youngest children ended up having the same father but yet the other three children in the middle don't.

Well, when my mother first hooked up with my father she got pregnant with my oldest sister Lavon. Unfortunately their relationship didn't last long because at the time my father was already married to someone else; you can say he was a player.

After my mother and father's affair ended my mother moved on with her life and fell in love with another man whose name was also Walter; this Walter's last name was similar to my father's last name but spelled with a *G* instead of a *D*.

He was my mom's first husband and together they had my sister Bev; my mother's second born daughter. Somehow that relationship didn't work out so they ended up getting a divorce.

Again my mother moved on with another man and his name just so happened to be of all things also Walter. This man was my mother's second husband and they had two daughters together; my sisters Tonya and Lisa were born.

However, that marriage didn't last either, so they eventually got a divorce; somehow my oldest sister Lavon grew up thinking that Tonya and Lisa's dad was also her biological father.

Anyhow, again my mother moved on with her life but she didn't move forward; somehow she went backwards and ended back up with my dad Walter. She became my father's third wife and they created me of all people; # that's when I was born!

Ten years after I was born my mother was going through her change of life and got pregnant with my baby sister Vet. She was shocked because she thought at her age it was no way she could still have any more children. She would always say that "Vet came from outer space" and she nicknamed her Sputnik.

So now you have the whole story on how it is that the oldest child and the two youngest children all have the same biological father and the other three children in the middle didn't.

Somehow, I've always considered all five of my sisters my whole sisters; just because all of us didn't have the same father didn't mean that my other three sisters aren't my whole sisters! I look at it like this… we all came out of the same mother's "hole" so to me that makes us all whole sisters and not just half- sisters.

I've always felt that a person having the same mother is way more relevant and significant than someone just having the same father; however, this is only just my opinion on this matter!

However, I do have a half-sister named Carla; she's my father's first born child; her mother was the one who our Dad cheated on when he got my mother pregnant with Lavon.

Growing up, Carla and I spent lots of time together but somehow we became distance over the years; her first born son is my nephew Darrey and he has two younger siblings, my niece Lora and my nephew Bambi; Carla married their father Geo.

Moving on to my mother's side of the family; she was an only child therefore I didn't have any aunts or uncles from her side; her mother was named LaVenya and she passed away when I was only three years old. I was too young to remember anything about her but I was told that she died from colon cancer.

My mom's dad was my grandfather Dave and he played a huge part in my life and I looked up to him. He was like a second father to me; he had a couple of sisters that were also in my life.

One of his sisters lived in Indianapolis; her name was Ellen and her nickname was Tuff Titty! Everyone who knew her knew that she carried a long switch blade knife inside of her bra. She didn't take no mess from no one and would cut somebody in a heartbeat if they messed with her; luckily nobody ever did. She was the spitting image of Tyler Perry's character named Madea.

Tuff Titty also cared for this little white girl named Teri; I'd enjoyed helping her babysit every time we visited. Teri was so pretty and I loved combing her long blonde hair; she looked like a little baby doll and I often wonder whatever became of her...?

My grandfather's other sister's was Mary Alice but everyone called her Achkels; she lived in Kentucky and her house was right across the bridge from Cincinnati. My parents visited her on plenty of occasions and it was always exciting going over there.

Achkels was born with a veil over her face; meaning that she had a special gift and could communicate with the spirit of a dead person's ghost; she would be able to reach that person especially if she had any prior connections with them.

Achkels never had any children of her own but adopted in the family a girl named Zetta, who married a man named JM. They had three boys together named Terry, Phil and Jonathan. I'd enjoyed visiting them because they were always nice, sweet, down to earth people; Zetta and her husband weren't fake people!

I remember going on road trips with them; I'd be sitting in the back seat with her two oldest boys doing all sorts of mischievous things to them boys until somehow I made one of them cry.

When our parents tried to find out what was going on, I would pretend to be so innocent as if I'd did nothing. Knowing all that time that I was the one who made them poor boys cry.

However, I don't know what made me do such terrible things to those boys at such a young age...? I guess I must have had some little boy issues even back then. Sorry Terry and Phil.

Other members of my mom's family that I grew up with were her cousins Migger, Sandy, Marylyn, Andrew J, Larry and Donald.

My mother's cousin named Bobby and his wife Francis would always come to visit us and Francis would always wear her blue wig; I was told that "their house in Peoria Illinois was right next door to where the late great comedian Richard P grew up at."

Another one of my mother's cousin's name Fry was a great inspiration to me! Fry inspired me to liking to travel and taught me how to read my first road map; she also taught me that it was a great big world out there that needed to be explored. Thanks Fry!

My mother also has an Aunt named Elizabeth; a few years ago she celebrated her one-hundredth birthday; however, I'm not sure if I want to live to I'm a hundred...? I guess it all depends on what shape I'm in if I live to be that age...?

Let's talk about my father's people now; his mother was named Lula and my dad was her oldest son. My father has two younger brothers; my Uncle Sea and my Uncle Jay.

My father dropped out of school in the ninth grade after his dad passed away; he helped take care of his mother in her time of need and also helped raise his younger brothers.

Uncle Sea was the next oldest after my father; he married a woman named Alley. They had two children together, my cousins CJ and Nee-Nee; he also has another daughter named Dixon.

Uncle Sea raised his family in Milwaukee for most of their lives; I loved visiting them and enjoyed when they visited us. One reasons why I loved visiting them so much was because of my cousin CJ. When I was around nine years old I had the biggest crush on him; somehow I was in love with my own first cousin!

Let's move on to my other Uncle Jay and his family; he married a woman also named Alley; they had two daughters together my cousins Alisa and May. They lived down the street from our house in a two family house along with my grandmother.

I remember when there were times when my Parents, Aunts and Uncles use to get drunk upstairs at my grandmother's house while I played downstairs with all my cousins having lots of fun. Alisa and May had every toy a child could dream of and more!

We would play for hours until our parents started cussing, fussing and fighting; that's when I knew my fun was over and it was time to pack up and go back home; # such a bummer!

Years later, one of the hospitals in the neighborhood needed the land their house sat on so they ended up moving to another neighborhood; this time my uncle and grandmother moved into separate houses within walking distance.

Uncle Jay moved his family into a very beautiful house and as the old saying goes, "he was always trying to keep up with the Joneses"; he wanted nothing but the best for his family. However, I always felt that he thought that he was so much better than my father was; I even heard him say once that "my dad wasn't shit".

However, when I was a little girl he treated me like I was one of his own daughters. When I moved into my first apartment sometimes I'd let him take women there just to have his affairs!

Somehow our relationship changed after the passing of my grandmother and that's when I first saw Uncle Jay for his true colors! However, before she passed away she often told me plenty of stories about him, Aunt Alley and my cousin Alisa.

One story was sometimes they'd sneak into her house in the wee hours of the morning thinking that she'd be sound asleep. However, one night when they came in she was wide awoke. Once they realized she was awoke they hid behind her curtains.

My grandmother said "she knew it was them because she recognized their shoes sticking out from underneath her curtains". However she had no idea why they were sneaking into her house.

When I'd mentioned these things to my uncle he'd just say "oh your grandmother's just senile." However, I felt that my grandmother was not senile; she was one hundred percent in her right mind and I believed everything she told me about my Uncle!

As far as his daughters are concerned my cousin Alisa and I had an ok relationship growing up. I even babysat for her first born son.

However, Alisa has another son that I never got the chance to know anything about; # to me that's just sad. ☹

Somehow Alisa and I relationship grew apart when we reached adulthood. I remember the time when she invited my baby sister to her house but never invited me; I never expected her to because I always felt that I wasn't good enough for her!

As far as her younger sister May is concerned I never got the chance to become close to her or know anything about her; I don't even know if she ever had any kids or not. When she got married she didn't even invite me, Lavon or Vet to her wedding. However, somehow Bev got invited but yet she's not even the blood cousin. How was that even possible…?

Well, I guess it ain't that kind of party! Somehow I always felt that I wasn't good enough for Uncle Jay's children; they look down at me like I'm some kind of trailer park trash or something.

Meanwhile, after my grandmother passed I think her spirit started to haunt Uncle Jay. He often told my mother that he heard strange noises whenever he went into my grandmother's house; he thought maybe it was squatters hiding out in there.

Uncle Jay went out and bought himself a gun. However, my mother told him that "no amount of guns was going to save him from his dead mother coming back to haunt him for all the wrong that he had done to her over the years".

Meanwhile, Bev was looking for somewhere to live and Uncle Jay rented out my grandmother's house to her. However, I don't think he rented it out to be helpful to her; I think it was only because he was just too scared to go back inside the house by himself! After Bev fixed up the house and made all the big repairs Uncle Jay put her out and sold the house. # Low down shame!

However, the main thing that pissed me off concerning my Uncle was when I wanted something of my grandmother to remember her by; he came over my house and took back the couple of things that I had taken for a keepsake. # Lowdown!

The day he arrived his arm was in a cast; he had the nerve to ask me to hold the door open while he struggled to carry out the things

I'd taken; apparently he didn't want me having nothing that belonged to my grandmother; damn him for being so selfish!

That just goes to show that all family members don't always be on the same page as the rest of us! According to some of the things I heard growing up about some of my kinfolks I can say that a few of them had some really serious issues back then!

Let's take for instance one person was well known for her famous chili and spaghetti recipe; she added this very special ingredient to it; however, I don't mean this in a good way!

This ingredient was so gross that you may not believe me when I tell you; it was her blood and not the blood from her veins; it was the blood from her monthly period; # (you didn't hear me!)

Allegedly she'd been feeding her husband her menstrual blood for years; I guess this ritual was some kind of voodoo shit..? Supposedly feeding someone their period blood is supposed to guarantee that the person that ingests the blood will never leave the person that gave it to them! Maybe somehow this ritual may have worked...? Going by the things that I witness over the years!

Meantime, another person served time in the penitentiary for a crime he committed; however, more time was added to his sentence because he was caught red handed having sex with a farm animals on the prison grounds! It's been said that "a sheep does have very similar sex organs as the human female"! # Wow!

I also heard that "one of my father's ex-wives was some kind of witch; supposedly she knew how to put spells on people!" Until I had kids of my own I never thought much about this; however they told me about some disturbing dolls they saw in her closets!

They saw these dolls that weren't just any ordinary dolls; these dolls resembled certain family members and had pins sticking out of them! What kind of shit was that...? I really don't know what to think; all I can say is I never trusted that woman!

Meanwhile, I also heard that someone in the family may have allegedly played a part in their own parents and aunt's deaths; I say this only because of certain circumstances that involved him during the times of these three peoples passing.

Let's take for instance, this person's father appeared to be doing just fine up until he gave him a cup of coffee; somehow right after he drunk the coffee he got really light-headed and dizzy so later he went to bed; somehow that next morning he was dead!

His father passed away sometimes in his sleep and to this day no one knows why he died; for some reason he didn't want an autopsy performed and immediately had his dad cremated.

When his Aunt was put on life support everyone wanted to leave her on it but this person allegedly had them pull the plug and take her off of the life support; not long after that while being under this person care somehow his mother ended up dead too!

So here we go again; I feel that this person may now be responsible for not one, not two but three people's deaths! I'm also keeping in mind that allegedly this person was in a lot of debt and really needed the money that his parents left him in their Will.

Not to mention all the other circumstances that surrounded these three people's deaths! So to me all these circumstances makes this person a # number one suspect in my book!

Who really knows what a person would do for money or how far they're willing to go to get it...? All I can say is God will judge him on his judgment day for whatever he did or didn't do...?

Enough hearsay; let's move on to all the other relationships I had with the people I came in contact with throughout my life. My first boy crush started at age six; with a country boy named Peter who I ran around barefoot with while visiting family in Tennessee.

However, I grew up a daddy's girl and I cherished everything about my father! I would follow him to the ends of this earth and often road in the car with him even when he was pissy drunk.

My father taught me how to drive a car when I was only nine years old; he'd let me sit on top of his lap and drive whenever he was in no condition to do so himself and that was quite often!

My father loved going to the race track and betting on the horses. One day on our way going to the race track my father was drinking and for no reason he started arguing with my mother.

The more that they argued was the more the car started swerving out of control. I begged and pleaded for him to stop but things only got worse and the car kept going over the yellow lines.

I was so scared that we were going to have a wreck but somehow I managed to jump out of the car while it was still speeding down the highway. I just couldn't take it whenever my parents argued and fought; # it took a toll on me and I hated it.

After I jumped out the car I rolled and landed on the guard rails. God must have caught me that day because I came out without a scratch; I got up off the ground and ran up this big hill.

After my father pulled the car over my mother started screaming for me to come back; but I just kept running up that hill. I remember thinking, I never wanted to come back! # What for!

Meantime, the neighborhood I grew up in was called Avondale on a street called Harvey Avenue. My household included my five sisters, my parents, my grandfather Dave and our landlord Brad. Also a lady named Miss Copeland and her daughter Pamela Jean lived in my household.

Miss Copeland and her daughter lived on the third floor of our house in a one bedroom apartment; however they had to go through our house to get to their apartment on the third floor.

Pamela Jean was only a year or two older than me and we might as well been sisters; the two of us became really, really close and I remember when we used to spy on my older sisters.

We would hide behind the sofa and take notes whenever my sisters had their boyfriends come over; we would always write down everything they said and did. I guess we were preparing ourselves for when it was our time to sit on the sofa with a boy.

However, I always felt sorry for my dear friend Pamela Jean because of how strict her mother was; every morning when she got ready for school her mother did some kind of counting thing.

Miss Copeland gave Pamela Jean until the count of five to have her socks put on; if she didn't have her socks on by the end of that countdown Pamela Jean would get a beat-down!

Not only was it a countdown for her to put on her socks; it was also a count-down for everything that she did; it didn't matter if it was putting on clothes, washing dishes or going to the store.

However, Pamela Jean never had anything completed by the end of her countdowns and this lead to many, many beatings for my dear sister-like friend; # enough of that counting please!

I hated hearing her mother doing that countdown every morning; hearing her screaming to the top of her lungs made me angry! She got beat on like she was some kind of punching bag or something; however, this made me stop liking her mother.

However, I was helpless and there wasn't a damn thing that I could have done to help her; I wished back then it was a 241-KIDS number because I would have definitely called it. What her mother did to her was straight up child abuse and that's a fact!

Eventually Miss Copeland and Pamela Jean moved out of our house into an apartment building three doors down from us. Our landlord rented out the third floor to my sister Tonya after they moved out. I shared some really great times hanging out with my sister up on that third floor; it was my home away from home.

Meantime, Pamela Jean's mother sent her away to a foster home and somehow we lost contact for a little while. One day she came home for a visit and we went to Kentucky with my parents. We walked to the store and on our way walking back somehow there was this car full of boys that were following right behind us.

Those boys followed us every step we took; they tried to get us in the car with them but we ran down a one way street to get away from them. Luckily, Kentucky had lots of one way streets; other than that they would have probably caught up with us!

However, we finally ditched them but I don't know what would have happened if those boys would have caught us...? I can only imagine that they would have definitely tried to rape us!

Meantime, my grandfather made me do what he called work details; a work detail was when I had to get down on my hands and knees and pick up every little crumb that was in our carpet.

Back then it wasn't about running any vacuum sweepers; somehow I was the human vacuum sweeper! However, picking up those crumbs made me feel like I was in a field picking cotton!

If I left one little crumb in that carpet my grandfather would go outside and find a tree branch to make himself a good switch; then he'd come back inside and tear my ass up! Needless to say he always made damn sure that our house stayed spotless!

My parents rented out our house from a man named Brad; he came with the house like some kind of package deal. My mother prepared all of his meals and every day my sisters and I would take turns taking him his breakfast, lunch, dinner & snack.

Brad's room was right next to my parent's bedroom; however I slept in the same bed with my parents until I was seven or eight years old. When I finally got my own bed they put it in their room.

I cherished my first bed and it was very special to me; I'd go to sleep every night and pretend that the gold buttons inside the white leather headboard were real gold. I'd make believe that one day I'd be able to cash in those gold buttons for a lot of money!

I remember sometimes being woke up in the middle of the night by noises that I had no idea what they were; I'd hear my parents whispering and my mother was always asking for tissue.

Back then, I didn't have a clue on what I was hearing or why my mother was always asking for tissue; looking back on it now it makes perfect sense; those noises I heard were them having sex. However, I didn't figured that out until I started having sex myself.

Growing up my mother never sat me down and explained anything about the birds and bees to me. Everything that I learned somehow I learned it on my own or from my four older sisters!

However, some of the things that I learned from them weren't always the right things! Especially when it came to dealing with the opposite sex; they taught me how to play mind games!

My sisters knew how to get revenge on the boys that betrayed them; one of the ways that they got revenge was with the Cun-say-dist. I guess you're wondering what that is…? Well it was this booby-trap that my sisters made up out of coat thread.

They would string the coat thread all over every bush and tree that was in our front yard. At night they'd call over the boys that they wanted to get back at. However, by it being so dark outside the boys couldn't see the booby-trap waiting for them.

They'd walk right into the Cun-say-dist and unfortunately they got cut-up from all that coat thread. I know it may have been a cruel thing to do but some of them boys really deserved it.

Growing up my sisters had lots of boyfriends and knew lots of guys; some of them were some real live characters. One guy called himself Pee-wee and he drove this big pink Cadillac.

Whenever he stopped by he couldn't cut off his car; if he did it wouldn't start back up. That pink caddy was a real live hoopty and it's a good thing that gas was cheap back then! Pee-wee needed to go somewhere and find himself a good mechanic; but somehow he thought he was this big baller or something! However, as Tamar Braxton would say # "boy go get your life"!

Another character that I remember back in the day was this old white man that made his own money; he made counterfeit twenty dollar bills. However, even I could tell that the money was fake; the heads on the presidents were entirely too big. I don't know how he ever passed those fake bills off...? # beats me!

My sister Lisa dated this guy named Greg; he'd always bring along his friend called Poochie. Although he was much older than me I still had the biggest crush on him! He had this head full of beautiful hair and for some reason I loved guys with lots of hair.

Meantime, I'll never forget the time that Lisa and Tonya had the biggest fight ever; it was over a boy no doubt. I remember trying to break them up and I thought that my oldest sister would help me but for some reason she just let them fight it out instead.

Meanwhile, my father was a good provider and did whatever was necessary to take care of the family! However, it was times he didn't have enough money to buy groceries; he was fortunate enough to have a couple of good friends that owned their own grocery store that he could go and get groceries from them.

One of his friends was a man named Mr. Eddie; his store was in an area called Walnut Hills and my father was able to get groceries anytime we needed them and Mr. Eddie would tell him to take his time on paying him back. Thanks Mr. Eddie!

My father also knew another store owner downtown that stayed open 24 hours; every weekend he'd pick up food for a dish that we called our "Dutch lunch"; this dish was a tray with all kinds of different cold cuts, cheeses, sardines, pickles and more...

The whole family ate this dish every weekend and we would stay up all night and watch the all night TV show hosted by Bob Shreeve; I remember those times as being the good ole days.

My father also knew a man that owned his own bar; he was able to get whiskey on credit whenever he wanted it; however, this man was the father of the famous lady named Doris Day.

Miss Day became well known for her song "Que Sera Sera, whatever will be, will be, the future's not ours to see, Que Sera Sera". However, I'll never forget that famous song because the meaning was so true; back then my future wasn't mines to see!

My father also knew the man that played the first original Tarzan from the television series featuring Tarzan, Jane and the monkey Cheetah.

Speaking of television shows; I loved watching the Uncle Al and Captain Wendy Show; I also liked the Mickey Mouse Club and all the movies with Annette Funicello and Frankie Avalon.

Meanwhile, my mother bought a piano and made all my sisters take piano lessons; however, their teacher was very mean and strict. I was so happy that my mother sold the piano before it was my turn to take lessons; thank goodness I dodge that bullet.

Meantime, my grandfather loved him some young ladies; he'd often dated women the same ages as my sisters. He fell deeply in love with a young lady named Veronica; she had four children; 3 girls and 1 boy and they're names were Linda, Johanna, Brenda and Ronald. # Shout out to all of them.

Johanna and Brenda were around the same age as myself; we became very close and hung out together. One day they invited me to go swimming but I didn't know how to swim; I just sat on the side of the pool and watched everyone else swim.

As I was sitting there minding my own business; out of nowhere this bad ass little boy suddenly pushed me into the pool. I'll never forget when I sunk down to the bottom of that pool.

After I floated back up to the top I was devastated, angry and didn't know what to do! I didn't know if I wanted to cry or go find the boy that pushed me so I could beat the crap out of him! Somehow this incident affected me in such a way that it caused me to never learn how to swim; but I still like getting in the water.

Meanwhile, my grandfather opened his own little restaurant and bakery; he sold all kinds of goodies, cakes, cookies and pies. I guess that's why I became a junk food junky over the years!

My grandfather eventually moved out of our house and moved in with his girlfriend; sometimes after he left Lisa decided to move her bedroom downstairs in his old room.

Lisa was six years older than me and I loved going downstairs playing with her; we would jump up and down on the bed pretending like we were in a gymnastics class; she taught me how to do summer saws and flips. She was my favorite sister growing up in the household and I definitely looked up to her.

Meantime, one night while Lisa and I were downstairs sleeping our next door neighbor called and woke up everybody in the house; he said some man was peeping in our window and watching us sleep! However, our neighbor went outside with his shot gun and chased that crazy pervert away!

Meantime, shortly after the peeping Tom we got a phone stalker. Some guy would call our house every night and just breathe on the phone. This went on for at least six months before it finally stopped. Somehow for some reason I can still remember that phone number from way back then # 861-9577.

However, the weirdest thing that happened in the neighborhood was when a bunch of wild animals escaped from the Cincinnati Zoo and were running loose in our back yard.

Our house was right down the street from the Zoo and I remember overhearing my mother and sisters saying look outside at the monkeys and the zebra in our back yard. Say what...

Moving on to my neighbors; I grew up next door to a family called the Millers; they were this family of seven boys and they had one sister named Yalonda who later in life was murdered.

The Miller family was the complete opposite of my family; they were a family of all boys with ten dogs; my family had all girls and twelve cats. However, I only liked one of their dogs named Mingo; he was this very smart, beautiful, German Sheppard.

However, there was always so much drama between the two families. It was pure chaos 24/7; girls against boys, cats against dogs but somehow we all managed to survive the madness!

Across the street was a foster care house with kids always coming and going; children from all walks of life lived there with all sorts of problems and issues; one girl was in a real bad fire and her face was badly burned; I remember feeling really sorry for her.

Also there was these two guys that had a crush on Lisa and I; we borrowed their record *"Me and Mrs. Jones"* by Billy Paul because that was one of our favorite songs back then. However, Lisa and I never did give them boys back their record. Sorry boys!

Other next door neighbors were the Harpers; Mom Lois and dad Ernest and their two children Bonnie and Ronnie. Also their grandparents Mr. & Mrs. Jones lived downstairs from them in a two family house. Mr. Jones had a talking parrot named Polly; we had to be very careful whenever talking around her because she would repeat everything we said and it didn't matter what it was!

The Harper family became a big part of our family and also lifelong friends; our mother's often went out clubbing together. Bonnie was around my sisters ages and Ronnie and I were the same age; we called ourselves cousins and we were very close.

However, my sister Bev somehow thought that Ronnie and I should have been a couple; when we were around nine years old she tried to give us a fake wedding ceremony; I got really angry with my sister because Ronnie and I were just like blood cousins!

Meanwhile, Ronnie and I made up this crazy Tarzan call; we would holla it out the window to get each other attention whenever one of us was on a punishment and couldn't talk on the phone.

Somehow we became partners in crime and we started sneaking into landlord Brad's room. One day we discovered something hiding inside his closet that was very shocking...

Landlord Brad had stacks upon stacks of cash in his closet. It was so much money that it was stacked all the way to the top of the ceiling; we couldn't believe our eyes after seeing all that cash!

I guess our Landlord didn't believe in putting his money into banks back then; I guess all the rent money that my parents paid him over the years must have been stashed in that same closet.

We started helping ourselves to his money on a regular basis! However, we helped ourselves to his cash for a long time before he finally realized that someone was ripping him off.

One day we went inside the closet and somehow all the money was gone; I guess he finally got wise and decided to put his money in the bank or somewhere else safe.

However, I used some of that money to buy me this long purple coat; on the back of it was a big, bright, yellow brick road which led to a castle just like in the movie the "Wizard of OZ". Whenever I wore that coat people would always say "follow the yellow brick road". However, I hated getting all that attention wearing that coat because back then I was just so damn shy!

When my parents asked me how was I able to buy that coat I lied and made up this story about me being in some kind of school program that paid their students cash money; # yeah right!

I guess Brad never mentioned anything to my parents about someone stealing his money because they never said nothing to me about it. All I can say is Lord forgive us for stealing his cash!

Meanwhile, the family that lived next door to the Harper's were the Tee's. Once a year Mr. Tee threw block parties for all the children in the neighborhood. I really enjoyed going to his parties; he'd barbeque and had lots of goodies for all the kids.

Mr. Tee also threw adult parties every summer; these party were called his "Heaven and Hell party." My parents would always tell me how much fun that they had going to one of these parties.

Once Mr. Tee's guest arrived he would have them draw a piece of paper from out of a hat and on these papers it would have either Heaven or Hell written on them.

If someone picked Heaven they'd go upstairs where it was nice and cool. However, if they picked Hell they'd go downstairs to his basement where it was hot because no air was turned on.

His upstairs was decorated like you were really in Heaven; everything was well lit up and very beautiful. He served all kinds of good foods such as steaks, lobsters and all kinds of fruits and everything you could think of. All of his alcoholic beverages were served as mixed drinks; such as Virgin Mary's, Piña Colada's, Slow Gin Fizzes and any kind of mixed drinks that you wanted.

However, if someone picked Hell and went to the basement it was very dark with only red lights. Downstairs in Hell he served all kinds of hot and spicy foods. All the alcoholic beverages were straight whiskey and no pop (soda) or juice was aloud in Hell.

At midnight everyone could then go anywhere in the house they wanted and it all became one big party. I remember I couldn't wait until I could attend one of those Heaven & Hell parties.

Meanwhile, Mr. Tee had a daughter outside his marriage named Anna who came to live with him after her mother died. Allegedly one day Anna came home from school and found her mother dead on their kitchen floor; someone had murdered her!!

Mr. Tee was so happy when Anna came to live with him; however, his wife wasn't so happy! Anna and his wife didn't always see eye to eye on things and they never got along. It seemed like her step-mom didn't want to see her happy!

Her step-mom was always so mean to her and she tried to throw a wrench in everything she did but that didn't stop Anna from doing whatever she wanted; we became really close friends!

However, I always felt that Anna had it made living with Mr. Tee; she never wanted for anything. I use to look at her father as being a very wealthy man; he always wore these nice suits and ties and drove these expensive cars along with having a fabulous home! Sometimes I use to wish that Mr. Tee was my father too.

Anna was just a couple of years younger than me and I loved going over her house and having sleepovers. However, I remember her being a little on the promiscuous side and sometimes she had a way of talking me into doing certain things!

One night she talked me into helping her practice how to kiss properly; she wanted to learn how to kiss so when the time came to kiss a boy she would already know how to do it right.

At first we started off by using pillows to practice on; then somehow we practice on each other. Back then she was the first person that I'd ever kissed in the mouth other than my parents!

Next door to her house was the apartment building where Pamela Jean and her mother moved to. Also in the building were two other families; the Mangrum's and the Smiths. I became close with a girl named Darlene and her sister Natalie; also a girl named Renee and her two brothers Gerald and Sonny; # hey what's up!

Next door to them lived Pamela Jean's cousins Patty and Carolyn. I always felt that they were some kind of geniuses because they had very high IQ's; they were very smart and their dog Princess was even smart. On the next street over lived a guy named Tom J who later in life became a well-known disc jockey.

Also in the neighborhood was a boy named Danny; we would always call on him whenever one of our cats passed away and he would always perform their funeral ceremonies for us!

Danny buried one of our cats named Robert- E'lla- Fontainous-Caborous- Philosopher- Condilious- Junior. He buried him deep into the ground in our backyard; however, somehow that next day the cat's paw was sticking out his grave!

Meanwhile one day, I found another cat and named her Heather; she was in a ball park and was very thirsty. My dad lured her into the car by giving her some beer. One day I found Heather dead wrapped around the clothes line pole in Ronnie's back yard; I never found out who or what killed my cat...? God bless Heather.

Meanwhile, moving on to my school years… the first school I attended was Rockdale Elementary. In kindergarten is where I first learned about bullies; a girl in my class named Renee bullied on me for no apparent reason; # she was a straight up hater!

For some reason this girl didn't like me; I never understood why because she was way bigger than me and I never did nothing to her. I was always the very shy, timid, quiet, skinny kid that hardly ever talked to anyone but yet somehow I still got bullied on!

Meanwhile in the first grade… I had a cat named Jody who followed me to school every day and waited for me to come out. He was a big orange cat that looked just like Garfield and he was very smart and acted as my protector; he didn't like anyone messing with me and most of the kids were afraid of him!

One day I never saw Jody again! However, my father said "he took him for a ride"; at least that's what he told me! Perhaps Jody got hit by a car and my parents didn't have the heart to tell me! That would have made more sense than him taking the smartest cat I'd ever had for a ride. However, God bless Jody!

Meanwhile in the second grade… is when my front tooth got chipped and I'll never forget the day it happened. My class was coming back from recess and everyone started running wild in the hallway; somehow I got pushed down and my front tooth hit that hard concrete floor! I can still remember the pain I felt. # Ouch!

By the time I reached the third grade… my teacher tried very hard to get me out of my shell. I was so quiet and shy that I hated whenever my teachers made me speak in front of my classmates!

In fourth grade… my teacher's name was Mrs. Bul Walston; she was a member of the Oakley Methodist Church and she gave her entire fourth grade class their own personal Bibles! Every day she also gave her class milk and cookies just like in kindergarten; however, we all looked forward to getting those snacks every day!

Also in the fourth grade… I had some sort of a speech defect and I had to take a speech class. However, the only thing that I can remember learning in that class was to keep my tongue behind my teeth whenever I talked. I guess maybe I was tongue tied or talked like Cindy Brady from the "Brady Bunch"...?

In the fifth grade... my teacher Miss Murrey put my desk right next to hers in front of the whole classroom and the other students teased me and called me teacher's pet. I remember going to her house on the weekends and spending the nights.

Miss Murrey adored me; however I didn't like her showing me any favoritism in front of my classmates. It made some of them jealous but I do thank her for always making me feel special.

In the sixth grade... I remember winning first prize at a sock hop contest. Although I was very shy I still loved going to those school dances. Students would dress their socks up and the person that had the best dressed socks was crowned the winner.

I won the contest probably because I was original and unique; I pinned all my mother's sparkling jewelry all over my socks and no one else in the entire school thought to do that.

In junior high... I attend a school called Samuel Ach. There were rumors going around about the school being haunted; it was supposed to be built over an old ancient Indian burial ground.

Rumor had it that the ghost of a girl named Molly was haunting the girl's locker room in the gym; several people claimed that they experienced encounters with the ghost of Molly.

However, I always found a way of getting out of taking gym because I really hated it; I guess I didn't stick around long enough to have any encounters with the ghost. Years later the school was tore down; it no longer exist. # I wonder what happened to Molly?

Also in junior high... I was very good friends with a girl named Suzy; she came over my house one day after school and later that night my father was supposed to take her back home. However, my father ended up getting so drunk that she had to end up spending the night with us!

That night was one of the most embarrassing nights of my life and it was the first time that one of my friends ever witnessed just how dysfunctional my family really was! My father's behavior made me feel so ashamed that I wanted to run away from home.

Other good friends I had in junior high were Janice P, Linda F, and Pam H; those were all my girls back then. How you doing?

Meanwhile, my two sisters Lavon and Bev were both pregnant at the same time with my nephew's Mookie and Doug. Both of them had huge big bellies and shared the same bed.

However, they weren't the only ones in my family that was pregnant at the same time; somehow my mother got pregnant with Vet and my sister Lisa also got pregnant. Double the trouble!

A few years later my sister Tonya got pregnant with my niece and named her Robin; her name came from the song "Rockin- Robin" by the Jackson's Five's; Tonya loved that record.

Meantime, Bev moved out the house and married a man named Butch; he was in the service so they ended up moving to Texas; I truly missed my sister after she moved out of the house.

Meanwhile, the Rockdale Temple in my neighborhood was holding meetings forming the group Cincinnati Black Panthers; these meetings took place right before the Riots broke out.

Speaking of the Riots… this was the craziest and most outrageous situation that I have ever witnessed in my entire life! I'll never forget the day I sat on my front porch and watched all the ridiculous, horrible actions that took place in my neighborhood.

If any white person drove down the street they got a brick thrown through their window! It didn't matter if they were young, old, male or female! If they were white they got savagely attacked!

However, it didn't make no sense what so ever how this one little old white man got attacked; first they threw a brick threw his window and busted his head wide open; blood was everywhere!

Then they dragged him out of his car and brutality beat him! If that wasn't enough…they turned his car over and set it on fire! That poor man was just lying there left for dead; it was so terrible!

I remember feeling so sorry for him and wished there was something that I could have done to help him. However, if anyone helped any of the white people they'd also got a beat down!

The police were called but they were too busy responding to other calls in the neighborhood; I think the old man ended up dying in the middle of the street that day. So un-necessary & sad.

During the riots there was so much chaos going on; stores were broken into and vandalized; people were running around with stolen goods; cars were on fire and people were hurt and crying out for help! This was truly an unbelievable tragic event.

Meanwhile, shortly after Lisa gave birth to my niece Lee-Lee she ran away and join the Black Panthers. # Power 2 the people! I was around ten years old and I'll never forget how hurt I was after she left! Not only did she leave her baby behind she also left me!

I was so devastated and wanted my sister to come back home; after she left we didn't hear from her for a long while! Lavon and Tonya also eventually moved out and it seemed like all my sisters were leaving me behind and I was lonely without them!

However, having my baby sister and my niece somehow made it all seem better. I loved having those two babies in the house at the same time; it was like taking care of a set of twins.

However, my mother wasn't feeling the same; it became overwhelming for her to continue caring for two babies; every day she started complaining that she couldn't handle it anymore and she was going to call Lisa's father to come and get little Lee-Lee!

Somehow, I'd already lost little Lee-Lee's mom to the Black Panthers and it was no way that l was going to lose her too. On the day when Lisa's dad came to get my niece I tried to grab her out of his arms! I screamed please don't take her away from me!

However, my mother said it was for the best but I just kept trying to pull little Lee-Lee away from Lisa's father. I remember my mother grabbing me and holding me back and I was devastated and highly upset as I watched her go out the door! After she left I cried for hours and I hated Lisa's dad for taking her away from us!

Meantime, Lisa finally called home and I briefly spoke to her over the phone; however, she refused to tell me where she was or when she was coming back home!

Meanwhile, baby Lee-Lee was adopted by one of Lisa's father's relatives and she didn't get the chance to be raised around the rest of my family and to me that was just so sad! ☹

When Lee-Lee was around three years old I made the biggest mistake by telling her that Lisa was her biological mother and the mother that she thought was her mom really wasn't.

However, after I got older I regretted telling her that kind of information; she was way too young to understand or process it. I was young myself and didn't know any better; I just hope by me telling her that didn't cause her any drastic effects in her life…?

Meanwhile, Lisa quit the Black Panthers and decided to come back home and get her life together; she went away to college in New York and met and married a man named Ed.

They had a child together and my nephew Koonin was born. However, after Lisa finished college her marriage with Ed didn't last and she ended up coming back home to Cincinnati.

She got her own apartment in an area called Winton Terrace in an apartment complex called Garden Hilltops; although she had her own place she still decided to stay at our parent's house.

Meantime, at the age of thirteen I was still playing with paper dolls; I would play for hours but I didn't like the store brought kind. I'd made my own by cutting them out of the big catalogs books.

However, I was so embarrassed whenever somebody stopped by and I'd hide them under my pillow. I knew deep down inside that I was too old to be playing with paper dolls but it was easier for me to relate to them then it was relating to real people!

Meantime, Ronnie introduced me to a girl named Connie who lived across the street from us. I didn't know that she would become my very best friend but somehow she did. Connie was thirteen almost fourteen and she had a baby boy named Too-bee.

Connie came from a big family of five brothers and two sisters; we became so close that we were inseparable; like two peas in a pod. My mother hated the fact that we became so close!

My mother didn't want me hanging around her or having anything to do with her just because she had a baby at such a young age; my mother felt Connie was a bad influence on me!

However, in spite of my mother not wanting us to be friends we started buying the same clothes and dressing alike; we also wore our hair alike. Connie was the twin sisters I always wanted.

Meantime, my father's drinking started taking its toll on me! He was always constantly fighting with my mother; the situation got so bad that one day it became physical and he knocked out one of her teeth! After he did that it was time to take action!

I remember one night Lisa and I woke up from a deep sleep; we couldn't take him beating on her anymore and somehow we ended up knocking him down on the floor and started beating him!

We kept hitting him until we exhausted ourselves and then we returned to bed as if nothing happened. My father just laid on the floor the rest of the night because he was too drunk to get up!

The fighting between my parents didn't stop and it continued every time my father started drinking. With all the Hell going on in the household it started to become impossible to sleep at nights.

One particular night I ended up drawing blood from my father and he called the cops on me! It all started after he woke me up from fighting with my mother. I was standing in front of the window when he said that "he was going to knock me out the window if I didn't mind my own business and go back to sleep".

We started arguing and then he raised his hand like he was going to hit me! At the time somehow I had these big garden scissors in my hand and I stabbed him; when the police arrived he tried to have me arrested but I only stabbed him in self-defense!

He was taken to the hospital and had to have seven stitches in his chest. I stabbed him right above his heart and the doctors said "he was lucky that I didn't stabbed him one more inch below or it could have been fatal"; # I was lucky that I didn't go to jail.

Meantime, my mother was very superstitious; she believed whenever our landlord ate those long peanuts in the shell that somehow the police would come to our house; she called the peanuts bad luck! However, it did seem like every time he ate those peanuts somehow the police would show up at our door!

Meanwhile, I was at a turning point in my life and I was no longer daddy's little girl; I had turned team mommy! I wanted to do something about my father's drunken situation so Connie and I decided to take up a karate class!

I wanted to be ready just encase my father tried to beat up my mother again. We stayed in the karate class long enough to learn the basics of how to defend ourselves. However, due to circumstances beyond my control Connie and I ended up having to leave the class before we finished it out in its entirety!

One day, our karate instructor Mike Posezey had us practice fighting with the other students in the class. When it came time for Connie to fight somehow it just didn't go according to plan!

The fighting session got totally out of control; at first Connie started off by using the karate skills that she'd learned but then the ghetto side came out of her and she went ham on the girl.

Somehow, Connie threw her opponent onto a pool table and hit the girl in the face with a pool stick. Our instructor broke up the fight and asked Connie to leave the class for good; of course I wasn't going to let her leave by herself so I ended up leaving too. However that was the end of us taking up karate; # it's a rap!

Meanwhile, I became close friends with another girl named JP and I met her one day in school when we both received an art award; art is what brought us together. JP started hanging with Connie, Pamela Jean, Anna and I; we all became best friends.

Meantime, Connie wanted me to meet her cousin Walden; he was the same age as us and I figured since he was her cousin that he couldn't be all that bad; his zodiac sign was Virgo.

My mother had a fit when she found out about him; it was bad enough that I was hanging with his cousin Connie. However, Walden and I cliqued from the very beginning; he was a sweet, loveable and caring guy and his parents raised him in the church.

However, just because Walden wore an earring in his ear and had a gold tooth in his mouth my mother felt he was no-good and labeled him as a thug. She didn't want to give him a chance less known the benefit of the doubt. The fact that he was Connie's cousin didn't help matters; it only seemed to make things worst.

However, I felt my mother's was being totally unfair because of her bad perception of him; she refused to believe that he was a decent and respectable young man!

Walden was my very first real relationship that I ever had with any other boy; however, in the beginning it was never sexual. We were very intimate with one another; we became inseparable!

I won't ever forget the time that he put these big passion marks all over my neck; my mother had a fit after she saw those hickies. I didn't try hiding the marks because I was the type that didn't like nothing touching my neck and Connie was the same way; we didn't wear turtle-necks or wear any kind of necklaces.

During this time I was turning fourteen and I still hadn't had my first period yet. My mother was getting concerned about my menstrual cycle not starting; she said all of my other sisters started their periods between the ages of nine and twelve.

However, I was so naïve back then that I thought a female couldn't have sex until she at least had her first period. I guess that's why I never tried to have sex with Walden. # Good for me!

Meantime, my mother found another reason to hate him even more then she already did; it was when my father offered him a drink of whiskey and Walden took him up on his offer.

He drank the whiskey down like a pro and my mother was furious! However, she was more outraged that he drunk the whiskey even more than she was about my father giving it to him!

This was the point when my mother really started hating Walden's guts; she wanted him as far away from me as possible. This was also when my father became really crazy about him!

However, I guess after Walden passed my father's little test and proved that he could handle his liquor; I guess somehow in my father's eyes he consider him to be a real man!

Meantime, I still hadn't had my period yet and I still thought I couldn't have sex until I got my first period; therefore I maintained my innocence and remained a virgin at the age of fourteen.........

CHAPTER 2

Memories and Events from Ages Fifteen---Twenty Seven

Life Gone Wrong

Hormones Gone Wild

Turning fifteen was a very difficult time for me; this was when destiny first started setting up different crossroads along with all kinds of conflicting paths! All I could do was buckle up for a ride of a lifetime and oh what a bumpy ride it was! # Rollercoaster!

I didn't know that almost a whole lifetime would somehow pass right by me; I had no clue what destiny had in store for me back then. Somehow it seemed like my life was on a fast track moving in a direction that I had very little control over.

However, after certain people interfered and tamper with my life was when it first started spiraling out of control. This caused my life to take a wrong turn down a path of self-destruction of no return and somehow my life ended up being capsize by all of this!

Fifteen seemed like a lifetime within itself; those twelve months felt more like twelve years. So many things happened in that one year it left me with a lifetime of hard ship and turmoil.

I finally received my first menstrual cycle but my mother still wondered why it started so late in my lifetime. However since my period started I thought it be ok to go ahead and have intercourse!

Like I said before my mother never sat me down and explained the birds and bees to me! Perhaps that was a good thing; otherwise I probably would have had sex at age thirteen.

Meantime, Lisa was still staying at my parents; she hadn't moved in her apartment yet. I planned on borrowing her keys so that Walden and I would have a nice place to go have sex at.

I took her keys without her knowing and Walden and I caught the bus out to her apartment. I wanted it to be really special; it was going to be my very first time ever having sex!

However, just because it was going to be my first time having sex didn't mean that it was going to be Walden's. He'd already lost his virginity to one of his distance family members. ☹

Although I didn't know what to expect somehow it didn't seem to matter. I truly loved Walden and wanted to spend the rest of my life with him. Little did I know it was never going to happen! However, I won't ever forget that red couch I lost my virginity on!

Of course the first person I told about me having sex was his cousin Connie; my best friend. I told her everything and we had no secrets between us and she knew everything about me!

Meantime, my mother still felt that Connie was a bad influence on me but really she wasn't; although she was the one who I experience smoking my first cigarette and first joint with. However, that was my own decision to do so; I wasn't a follower!

I'll never forget when she turned me on to smoking my first joint. I had no idea what to expect or how it was going to make me feel and I didn't know what kind of affects it would have on me!

I went next door to Ronnie and Bonnie's house and ended up getting on Bonnie's sewing machine trying to sew something. However, I really couldn't tell whether or not if I was high or what.

Somehow everything was so funny to me and for some reason I just couldn't stop laughing. I tried my best to keep cool so that Bonnie wouldn't suspect nothing or know that I was high.

I didn't dare want her knowing that I had smoked a joint; I was too afraid of what she might have thought about me getting high; however, I just kept laughing at anything and everything.

I guess she wondered what the hell was so funny; well now you know Bonnie I was high off my first joint. However, after my high wore off I became very hungry; the munchies had kicked in and I ended up eating some of everything that day!

Meanwhile, my mother had no idea that I wasn't a virgin anymore but somehow she still tried every trick in the book to break up my relationship with Walden; she wasn't going for it.

However, I always felt that on one hand Walden was this perfect Saint; but on the other hand he was this bad boy rebel. I always felt that somehow he was being torn between good and evil when it came to dealing with his parents and the Church.

Meantime, Connie developed this crush on Ronnie and they ended up dating; JP ended up dating Connie's brother Fluke and the six of us all started doing lots of things hanging out together.

Connie, JP and I called the fellows our three Mellows; we'd referred to them as mellow number one, mellow number two, and mellow number three. Somehow, we came up with this idea from the song by Jerry Butler called *"Understanding Mellow"*.

Meanwhile, Connie, Pamela Jean, JP and I started hanging with another girl named Sade; she too lived in our neighborhood. We all went to the same school and we became real good friends.

There was also another girl named BB and sometimes she hung around us too; however she also hung around another girl name Casey but none of our clique liked Casey very much.

Casey was the type of girl that was very two-faced; she tried to manipulate friendships! She was a big trouble maker and liked keeping up a bunch of confusion; a real live drama queen with loose lips that liked to sink battleships! However, that didn't stop us from becoming good friends with BB because she was cool.

We all attended a school called Hughes high school and we did lots of things together. I remember the thing that we did most together was skipping school; most of the times it was ditch time!

We called ourselves the Hells Angels and instead of going to school; we often caught the bus and went downtown to see a movie at these 2 theaters called the Regal & the State Cinemas.

Those two cinemas allowed students in during school hours without any questions asked; just as long as you had the price of admission you were more than welcome to attend those theaters.

On another occasion during school hours we needed somewhere to hang out; we ran into these two old men and we ended up hanging out with them. The whole time we rode around town with them somehow they were drinking and getting drunk.

However, these two men got into this big argument and the car kept going over the yellow lines. All of the sudden the driver stopped the car in the middle of the street and put the other man out of his car. Somehow the passenger door still remained wide open as the highly intoxicated man drove off at full speed ahead!

When the man stopped for a red light we all jumped out of his car; we didn't want to go any further after seeing that he was too incapacitated to drive! However, none of us was familiar with the neighborhood and we didn't have a clue of where we were at.

We stopped at a gas station to ask for help and they said that we were in a neighborhood called Cheviot. However, back then Cheviot was a predominantly white neighborhood; we didn't see not one other black person out on the street that entire day!

It started getting really late and we had to get home before our parents got suspicious. If we weren't home by the time school let out we knew we were going to be in some real serious trouble! As we looked for a bus stop we came across this house that had these three burning crosses sitting in their front yard.

We thought it was so strange seeing those crosses burning in that front yard. Then out of no-where someone yell out "y'all black ass niggers better get the hell up out of here right now!"

Then all of the sudden these big ass dogs came running towards us and we started running as fast as we could. However, the dogs weren't the only ones chasing us; so were all these men!

These men all wore long white hooded outfits with the eyes cut out of them. However, this was when we all realized that we were being chased by the Ku Klux Klan's & their killer Klan dogs!

The next thing we knew we were running for our lives! They chased us for about five or six blocks before they decided to stop running after us. However, this was all our first time ever being up close and personal with any members of the KKK; # really scary!

We finally found a bus stop and caught the bus downtown to get home. By then it was almost dark outside and we all looked forward to a good ass-whipping. On our ride home we came up with a story to tell our parents why we were so late getting home.

When Connie first got home she was really nervous; she'd left her baby on her mother to long after school was dismissed. She told her mother that we went to Frisch's to get a Big Mack. However, there was only one thing wrong with her story; Frisch's sold Big Boys and not Big Mack's; # busted.

After Connie was caught in her lie it caused her mother to call the rest of our parents to get to the bottom of what was really going on. Our parents compared notes and we all ended up on punishment. Back then it did take a whole village to raise 1 child.

Meanwhile, Hughes turned into a prison grounds and it was almost impossible to skip school anymore; everyday while classes were in session they had hall monitors patrolling the hallways.

They put chains on all the doors and no one could leave the building anymore without having permission. However, that wasn't going to stop us Hells Angels from still being able to leave school!

One day, Connie, JP, Sade, Pamela Jean and I, all decided to leave school early regardless of all the chains on the doors; we somehow came up with a master plan on how to accomplish this.

We checked the basement windows to make sure that they weren't locked; we knew exactly how we were going to escape! The plan was for everyone to meet in the basement after the first bell rung and it was then time to put our master plan into action.

Everyone starting climbing out of the window; first Connie, then Sade and then JP. Pamela Jean was still struggling to get out; however due to her weight she was always the slowest one.

As soon as Pamela Jean got outside somehow the hall monitor grabbed my sweater; he had a hold on me but I was able to escape him by taking off my sweater and leaving it behind.

After we got outside we went across the street to the Cincinnati University College. We always hung on the campus pretending like we were just one of the other college students.

That day hanging on campus we met this guy name Lackey. However, he wasn't a college student either; he only hung around the campus so he could try to pick up on the real college women.

Lackey and his friend Hall was older than us but that didn't stop them from trying to talk to us. However, I had no interest in either one of them; I was still head over hills in love with Walden.

Walden was my world and being with another guy was absolutely out of the question. Little did I know then, destiny was going to have Lackey somehow destroy a beautiful relationship!

Meanwhile, Hughes went on lockdown; they decided to nail all the windows shut. This was the point that we could no longer leave the building during school hours. It was over said and done!

Meantime, Lackey's friend Hall was interested in hooking up with Connie and somehow Lackey wanted to hook up with me! However, somehow they found out where Connie lived; and one day out of nowhere they just showed up at her house somehow!

Walden just so happened to be over there that day. Neither Connie nor I knew that they were coming; we didn't even know they knew where she lived; less known show up on her door step!

Lackey was well aware that I already had a boyfriend but that didn't seem to stop him from trying to get with me! He was also aware that Walden was my very first boyfriend I'd ever had!

I guess by me only having sex just a few times I was still like a virgin in Lackey's eyes! As far as he was concerned I was still young fresh meat and he planned on reeling me in as fresh bait!

He was four and a half years older than me; I was fifteen and he was nineteen almost twenty. He was born under the zodiac sign "Virgo" the same sign as Walden; what a weird coincidence!

Getting back to the day he and his friend unexpectedly showed up over Connie's house…Little did I know back then that somehow Lackey had his own agenda that day! He planned on breaking me and Walden up but somehow I never saw it coming.

When Connie first let them inside of her house we were up front watching television and Walden was in the back chilling with his male cousins and Lackey and his friend waited in her hallway.

I was curious to know how they found out where Connie lived so I went to confront them. As I stood there talking to them suddenly Lackey got real close to me. I told him to "back up off of me and asked him what the hell did he call himself trying to do"?

All of the sudden he grabbed me and pulled me closer to him. At first I couldn't figure out why he did that; but in that very split second out the corners of my eyes I saw Walden walk by.

Just as he walked passed was the exact same moment that Lackey's friend Hall grabbed my arms and held them tightly behind my back. However, Walden couldn't see Hall standing there because he was hiding behind some curtains; therefore he could only see Lackey and me standing in the hallway!

Somehow Lackey put his hands over my mouth so that I wouldn't scream; then he stepped on both of my feet with his feet so that I couldn't kick him; then he put his mouth over the top of his hands to make it look like I was kissing him. I tried my best to break free but the two guys were just too strong to get away from!

What Walden thought he saw wasn't the case. Although I was innocent it didn't look that way; however, he could only go by what he thought he'd saw and that was me kissing another man!

Walden was so upset that he turned around and went to the back of the house; then Lackey and his friend let me go free! It all happen so quickly that I didn't even know what hit me; somehow he was able to carry out his plan on destroying my relationship!

After I was set free I ran to him and tried to explain to him what really happened. However, he wasn't buying my story and he refused to believe anything that I had to say from that point on!

He just kept saying "he knew what he saw". However by that time it didn't matter anymore; it was nothing that I could do to convince him otherwise; what he saw wasn't what it looked like!

His heart was already broken and he wanted nothing else to do with me; although I was set up and held totally against my will somehow Walden still didn't believe me not one little bit.

In a matter of seconds Lackey destroyed my whole life. That just goes to show...you can't always judge a book by its cover. Everything that appears to be isn't always what it really is!!!

Where was my understanding mellow when I needed him the most...? In a blink of an eye my very first relationship was destroyed all because of someone else's wrongful intentions!

Meantime, I tried everything to win back Walden but nothing seemed to work. I tried calling him but he refused to take my calls; he told his sisters to tell me that he wasn't home. Somehow he just wouldn't understand that I too was a victim of circumstances.

Lackey meant nothing to me and I barely knew him; the only other contact that I ever had with him was the few conversations that we had on the college campus whenever I skipped school.

Meantime, I became really depressed about my break up; I tried everything to move past what happened. I started going out to parties and drinking and smoking weed a lot more often!

My girlfriends and I also started sneaking out of the house and hanging in this teenage club called the Psychedelic Grave. One night who of all people did we run into; it was Lackey himself. There he was up in the club slow dancing with some other female!

At first I couldn't believe my eyes; the man that destroyed my world in less than a minute was up in the club trying to pick up on some more young ladies. # Ain't that about nothing!

Meanwhile, I continued seeing him hanging in the club. I started thinking about all the trouble he'd gone through just to break up my relationship and somehow that made me think about going ahead and giving him a chance; sure why not...?

Whenever we saw one another at the club we made out. However, it was only just by kissing and grinding on each other; we never had sex! For one we didn't have nowhere to go have sex at; I definitely wasn't taking him home to my parent's house!

I remember onetime somehow he gave me his toothache; that was my first time knowing that someone else could give another person their toothache just by kissing them in the mouth.

Meantime, I didn't see him hanging in the Psychedelic Grave anymore; I guess he decided to move on elsewhere to go find somebody else that could provide him a place to have sex at.

Not only did he destroy my relationship with my first love he also left me hanging! He moved on all because I didn't come up with a place for us to have sex; to me that was just cold-blooded.

Meanwhile, Pamela Jean joined the Job Corp to get a break from her controlling mother. I remember writing her a letter while she was away; I mention in my letter about how I was feeling and how hurt I was over my situation between Walden and Lackey.

In my letter I also swore that I would never let another man hurt me ever again; I also made a solemn oath to become a player and vowed to never let my guard down and become emotionally attached to other guy for as long as I lived; yeah right!

Pamela Jean's mother must have gotten a hold of that very same letter and gave it to my mother sometimes over the years. However, I didn't know that my mother knew exactly how I felt about men back then. I never knew that she had that letter until later on down the line after she passed away and that's when I found that same letter amongst her personal possessions.

Meantime, JP wanted me to go with her to this party that someone in our neighborhood was having; I decided to go but deep down inside I was hoping that I'd see Lackey there!

On our way walking to this party JP was telling me about this guy named Tony that also went to Hughes. However, she didn't like dating guys that went to the same school as us; she liked dating much older guys that were outside of our school district.

JP said "the next time she saw this Tony that she was going to break up with him"; she said "her feelings for him weren't the same as his feelings were for her". However, according to JP "Tony was supposed to be head over hills in love with her"!

When we first arrived at the party I looked to see if Lackey might have been there but he wasn't; we decided to stay anyway and JP got the shock of her life; somehow Tony was at the party!

Although I'd never met this guy before somehow destiny was already setting up cross roads between us; however, back then I had no idea what destiny had in store for me and Tony!

JP introduced me to him and that was my first time ever meeting Tony! JP never expected to see him there especially after just saying that she was going to break up with him the next time she saw him; suddenly her words were staring at her right in front of her face and she was put in a very compromising position!

She tried to find the right moment to tell him that it was over between them; however, he didn't give her a chance before he turned the music down low and wanted to make some kind of special announcement...

JP and I stood there next to him after Tony got everyone's attention and suddenly the entire room became silenced; all of the sudden somehow it turned into an all eyes on us moment...

Everybody at the party stopped whatever they were doing; they all wanted to hear whatever he had to say. JP didn't have a clue on what he was about to say or do next. However, his big announcement was that he was dedicating a song to her.

Both of us thought that he was about to play a record for her; but instead he grabbed her hand and held it very tightly. I can't remember if he got down on one knee or not; all I know is it became a very serious, very dramatic and emotional moment.

Out of no-where Tony started singing this slow love song to JP. I can't remember if the song was someone else's song or if it was one he made up himself...? I do know that he sounded really amazing!!! That night it must have done something to me after hearing his soft, sweet, sexy, beautiful voice; I was so impressed!

However, JP was so uncomfortable standing there, and somehow by me standing next to her I could feel the same discomfort myself. All the attention that Tony caused made JP feel really embarrassed and somehow I felt embarrassed for her.

This was a very intense moment for JP and after Tony finished singing his heart out to her it became very difficult for her to move forward with her plan on ending things between them; however, this situation was uncomfortable and very awkward.

I myself couldn't believe that she still wanted to break up with him; especially after he'd just finished singing his heart out to her! Who knew that his voice was so enchanting & captivating..?

Although I'd just met him somehow I felt really sorry for him! I knew JP was about to break his heart and he didn't even see it coming, and that's something that I could definitely relate too.

JP said after she called it quits that Tony told her "one day he'd make it big and she would regret not sticking by him"! Boy did he make it Big... Oh well JP I guess you really blew that one!

However, this is the part of my story that gets a little fuzzy; I won't lie to you and I can only tell you what I think happened next... For some reason it's blocked totally out of my mind.

I can only assume what happened next as far as Tony and I are concerned. But one thing I do know for sure is sometimes after the night of that party somehow Tony and I got together!!!

I can't exactly swear how I ended up hooking up with him but my theory is; I do believe that it's possible that we made out in a closet that very same night of that party; I do need confirmation!

However, JP said she doesn't remember me ever leaving her side that night but apparently something went down; Tony and I started dating and for some reason we kept it on the down-low!

I don't know if the situation between us was supposed to be like the song that said "if your girl starts acting up then you take her friend"; but basically that's how it was; # on the rebound.

Meantime, we continued to keep our relationship a secret but I'm not exactly sure why we did; it really makes me wonder! Although I really don't remember just how we actually became a couple I do remember at some point I fell head over hills in love!

Somehow our relationship grew stronger and stronger each day; this was the point when I finally moved past the Lackey and Walden situation and moved forward with only Tony on my mind.

Tony was the second guy that I had a sexual relationship with; I must have been pretty desperate to be with him because I remember one day sneaking him into my parent's house!

I never once tried to sneak Walden or Lackey into the house! Therefore with that being said… it had to be something really special about Tony in order for me to take that kind of risk!

However, I think that was our first time being intimate with one another; not unless the first time was at that party…? Only Tony himself can give insight on what took place that night.

The first time he came into my house I was wearing my favorite wine colored bell bottom pants. I remember taking him up stairs to my parent's bedroom where my childhood bed still sat at.

Remember earlier when I mention about pretending that the gold buttons on my white leather headboard were real gold and I said "one day I'd cash them in for a lot of money". Well I laid down on that very same bed with Tony laying upon me! Who knew back then that I was lying with a future celebrity…? I sure as hell didn't.

The day that I took him into my house I didn't know where my parents were nor did I seem to care! I was so wrapped up into him that getting busted was far from my mind. He was definitely the definition of a true sweetheart and I fell really hard for his love!

I'll never forget how aroused he became; somehow he got so hard that he split this big ass hole down the crouch area of my favorite pants! However, by him being that powerful and breaking through my pants like that somehow it really frighten me!

I was still very new at the sex thing by me only just having that one other sexual experience with Walden! At that point I became concerned that Tony might be more than I was able to handle! I started wondering about what he could do to me once my pants came off and I was terrified by just thinking about it!

I guess I thought that all guys had the same size penises; one size fits all. Therefore it never dawned on me that guys had different size penises! However, little did I know back then that a penis could grow to be that damn big; # I remember it being huge!

As I laid there with him on top of me I remember thinking what the hell have I gotten myself into...? However, this was the point when I put all my fears aside; I relaxed and let go to enjoy this sweet, sexy and charming guy and size no longer mattered.

Not only did Tony have this head full of hair he also had this smooth, chocolate, beautiful complexion; along with a beautiful set of white teeth with one of the most amazing smiles ever.

I remember him being very affectionate and very passionate; his touch was so gentle that it made me feel so rejuvenating and safe! It was just something about him that seriously turned me on and set my soul on fire; he definitely made my temperature rise!

When he kissed me it made me get even hotter; and when he was on top of me it felt like my whole body was burning up inside; all I could think about was letting him get inside of me!

There was just something about him that made my desire for him really strong; also something about his voice that I loved. Not to mention how remarkable he sounded when he sung to JP.

Every time he smiled at me his smile lit up my day! It was just something about his eyes whenever he looked at me it made me want him even more! # I was hooked, lined, and sinker!

He wasn't anything like the other guys that went to our school. I remember him having this remarkable personality and he was so smart and much more mature than the guys his own age!

He had a very good head on his shoulders and he was highly intelligent; he was definitely a no-nonsense kind of guy! He was born under the zodiac sign "Gemini" and somehow we both were born on the seventh of a month; # Go Lucky 7's"

However, he didn't dress like the other guys his own age; he dressed for success even at age fifteen. I don't remember him too much wearing blue jeans or sneakers; I remember him mostly wearing dress pants, dress shirts with vest and dress shoes.

Guys like him were very hard to come by back then; he was all about taking care of business; he wasn't up for any bull and he was filled with all kinds of big dreams and ambitions. I'm not at all surprised that he ended up being so successful; # you go boy!

Meantime, this was the point when I put all my girlfriends on hold; I was so head over hills in love with Tony that I only wanted to spend all my time with him & him alone; forget those girlfriends!

Connie was the only one that I told about him; none of my other girlfriends knew anything about him! I guess the reason why I kept him a secret was so that JP wouldn't find out about us...?

I stopped catching the bus and walking home with all my girlfriends; when they'd asked me why wasn't I hanging with them anymore I would make up all kinds of lame excuses why not.

I remember every day after school he'd walk me home and carry all my heavy books on those long walks home. He was just the perfect gentleman in every way you could possibly imagine; he was so sweet and caring and he was a real live sweetheart.

Meantime, I knew I couldn't keep sneaking him into my parent's house to have sex; I thought of the perfect place for us to go. It was over my sister Tonya's place and we often hung over there because she lived right down the street from our school.

However, the only thing about going over her place was that she lived all the way at the top of this big old spooky Church. I remember it being lots of stairs before reaching the top. It was very dark and kind of creepy but just as long as Tony was with me I didn't care; I felt safe and secure being around him! Little did I know that I would conceive his baby in that very same Church!!!

Meanwhile, as time went by I noticed that I didn't have as much energy as I normally had. However, I had no idea that it was even the slightest possibility that I could have been pregnant.

By me not too long started my first period I knew nothing about any menstrual cycles or about any missed periods. I was so naïve back then becoming pregnant never even crossed my mind!

I remember sleeping all of the time and feeling different and some mornings I'd fill sick to my stomach and throw up! I didn't think much about it until my parents started noticing the change!

However it's funny; not that long ago I was just an innocent virgin still playing with paper dolls; therefore I knew nothing about the life that was starting to grow inside of me; the precious life that Tony left behind. However, my mother knew exactly what was going on and she knew I was pregnant but I didn't have a clue!

My mother discussed my situation with my father and all my sisters but kept me in the dark. Somehow I was the only one that didn't know that Tony had gotten me pregnant in that Church!

Meantime, one Saturday night my mother went to Bingo and I'll never forget that night. It was the night that I moved out of my parent's house; my father left me no other choice! I had to leave!

This was the point when I decided to go live with my sister Lisa. It all came about when my father woke me up from out of a deep sleep! I was downstairs sleeping when all of the sudden he started hollering and yelling at me for no apparent reason!

My father started saying "wake up, wake up all you do is sleep all the damn time". However, being woke up so abruptly I didn't know what was going on; I was lost, confused and clueless!

He started preaching things from the bible but to me it didn't make any sense why he was acting like that. I never saw him that angry before; not even the time when I stabbed him in the chest!

He then called me a "pregnant bitch" and hit me in the head with a broomstick and it broke in half; and my head swelled up! Although I heard him call me a pregnant bitch, for some reason it still never dawned on me that I was really pregnant. # Stupid me!

However, all I knew was that I had to get the hell up out of that house; so I packed all my clothes and called my grandfather to come and get me and take me over to my sister Lisa's house.

I knocked on her door and stood there devastated with all my suitcases crying like a little baby! Lisa was just about to have a romantic candle light dinner with her boyfriend Tribbles.

Although my father had been drinking didn't excuse what he did to me; it was totally uncalled for. Whether or not if I ever told Tony about any of this I really don't remember. Somehow I can't remember having anymore communications between us!

For some reason the last recollection that I have of him is our encounters at the Church; the church where we shared all those beautiful moments together that resulted in my pregnancy; the same pregnancy that at first I wasn't even aware of back then!

However, little did I know then that destiny was setting up another path later in my future; this would allow me to get another chance somehow to see Tony one more time again in my lifetime!

Meanwhile, after a couple of weeks passed my mother and my oldest sister came out to Lisa's house. However, this wasn't just a social call; this was more like an execution style visit.

Little did I know then...Destiny was about to change my entire future...My life was never going to be the same; I was going to hold major regrets for the rest of my life to come!!!

My mother was standing there with this little bottle of pills in her hands; she said "I had to take the entire bottle". When I asked her why I had to take them she said "because it was for my own good and because she said so; and I better swallow all of them".

I told her I didn't want to take any pills but she insisted; she said "by the end of the day I was going to take the whole bottle even if she had to cram them down my throat herself".

However, I still didn't know that I was pregnant with a child! When I looked at that bottle it contained one-hundred pills; I told my mother it was no way that I was going to swallow one hundred pills... Are you serious; is this some kind of joke or something...?

However, she crushed up the majority of the pills and added them into some hot water; she stirred them until they started to dissolve. My mom said "I better drink every drop"; then she picked up the glass and started trying to force the water down my throat.

She threatened me if I didn't drink the water containing all those pills that she was going to send me away to a foster home for bad girls; just like Pamela Jean's mother sent her away too.

However, I realized I didn't have much of a choice; I sure as hell didn't want to be sent to a girl's home so I slowly started drinking the water. I wished I wasn't so damn gullible back then!

I won't ever forget those little white pills; they were called Humphrey's Elevens! They destroyed my entire life and caused me to have regrets for the rest of my life!!! However, somehow I knew nothing good would ever come from taking all those pills.

Soon as my mother left I went into the bathroom and stuck my finger down my throat and tried to make myself throw up. I was only able to vomit some of the pills up but plenty had already gone into my system! Still not knowing I had a baby inside of me!

Later that night, I was feeling lost and confused; I started getting this real bad ringing in my ears and my stomach felt like it was in a million knots; I started cramping really bad and the cramping got so severe it was almost unbearable to deal with!

I thought maybe that I needed to have a bowel movement or something; so I sat on the toilet and tried to have one. The next thing I knew all this gushy looking stuff started coming out of me!

All this white, gross, bloody looking little pieces was falling into the toilet and at that point I was scared shitless. I still didn't know what this mess was that was coming out of me! Little did I know back then it was the baby that Tony had put inside of me!

I panic and started yelling and screaming for my sisters to come into the bathroom but Lavon didn't want to come in; Lisa ended up coming in and she immediately flushed the toilet.

Lisa called my mother and I heard her say "it's done". What's done...? However, I didn't have a clue on what she meant by that comment! By the time I figured it all out it was way too late!

My un-born baby had already been flushed down the toilet like a piece of shit and there was nothing that I could do about it. What was done, was done; my baby was gone forever and I had to live with this tragic thing that my mother forced me to do!!!

Meantime, JP still didn't know anything about Tony and me or the fact that he'd gotten me pregnant. What my mother forced me to do was going to remain my horrible secret forever; I buried that secret deep within my soul and kept it locked inside of me!

After everything was all said and done my mother warned me not to ever have sex with anyone! She threaten me again by saying if I had sex that she'd send me away to a foster home!

For some reason I still don't have any recollection of what happened between Tony and me; I do need to know what really happened between us! How did we break up; how did we depart our ways..??? Unfortunately I don't have any of these answers!

Whatever happened between us is still locked deep down within my soul. Only he has the key that will unlock all these un-answered questions that are still trapped deep inside of me!

Meanwhile, I started acting up and getting into a lot of trouble at school; especially in my ninth grade math class. I had the craziest math teacher ever and his name was Mr. Pal.

I took his class during lunch period and he treated our class like we were his prisoners. BB, Casey and I were in the same math class together and the three of us gave that poor man hell.

We only gave him a hard time because of how he treated his students; he made our class write a six line explanation on practically anything and everything that we did in his classroom.

Let's take for instance, if we had to use the restroom we had to write a six line explanation and tell why. However, having to use the restroom shouldn't have required any explanation at all.

BB, Casey and I would always write down stupid, crazy stuff because of how ridiculous our teacher was; he would get mad at us and tell us to stand in the corner for the remaining of the bell.

Whenever it was real hot outside he made us suffer; he didn't let us open up any windows. It could be burning up in that classroom but we still had to sit there in all that hot ass heat.

Every day he wore suit jackets with long sleeved shirts; he sweated so bad that it left these big wet stains underneath his arms. However, this caused him to carry a real bad body odor and sometimes it made the whole classroom smell really funky.

Mr. Pal always provoked us into doing something crazy! One day while everyone was still at lunch BB, Casey and I decided to pull a joke on him. The three of us chewed a lot of chewing gum and went back to our classroom and somehow we stuffed all that gum deep inside the lock on our classroom door!

When we returned from lunch everyone was waiting to get inside the classroom; but because of all the gum inside the lock it caused the door not to open. Somehow Mr. Pal knew it had to be either BB, Casey or me that caused the problem! He immediately sent all three of us straight down to the principal's office!

However, due to me always getting in trouble it caused me to fall way behind in math. I spent more time in the principal's office than I did in my math class so I ended up failing math.

I was taken out of Mr. Pal's class and placed in the basement in a slow-learning class for students with learning disabilities. However, whoever attended that class was called a Zeak and considered to be dumb; lots of people made fun of me!

While being in that classroom I met this guy named AP and he had a little crush on me; however this fellow classmate was always fighting with someone and I do believe that's why he was placed in that class; later in life he became a professional boxer!

Meanwhile, JP came to stay with Lisa and me because of some disagreement that she had with her mother; I still didn't tell her anything about Tony and me or that I'd gotten rid of his baby!

I had to be extra careful around her not to ever let her find out about the terrible thing that I was forced to do; I found myself grieving over my lost but somehow I still had to hide it from her.

I started hating myself and wanted to replace the baby that my mother made me kill. Getting pregnant again was very, very important to me! I guess I thought that if I got pregnant again that it would somehow help ease the pain that I felt deep inside of me!

Meanwhile, one day JP, Anna and I planned on going to the mall; however, that day we didn't have any intentions on stealing anything but somehow we ended up doing a little shoplifting.

JP and I were satisfied with what we'd already taken and we were ready to go home. Anna wanted to go in one more store and somehow we ended up going inside with her. That was a mistake!

JP and I noticed that someone inside the store was following us around and watching us; we knew not to take anything and we warned

Anna not to either; however, she was hard-headed and didn't listen to us and she ended up taking something anyway!

After we walked out of the store we were stopped by their security guard; he escorted us back into the store and searched Anna and JP's purses. That day I wasn't carrying a purse but JP had all my stolen stuff inside of her purse. After they removed all the stolen merchandise they called the police to come and get us!

When the police arrived they handcuffed us and took us to a juvenile detention center; when we first arrived at the center they made us take off all of our clothes and gave us a full body search.

We stayed in lockdown until our parents came to get us and we had to be back in court that next day. Anna and I went home but JP didn't; somehow her mother refused to take her home and decided to teach her a lesson and made her stay there overnight.

That next day the three of us had a court hearing to find out what our fate was going to be. Anna and JP were charged with theft but since I wasn't caught with anything in my possession I was only charged with being an accomplice to theft.

The judge put all three of us on house arrest for thirty days; back then they didn't have the ankle bracelets like they do now; it was totally the parent's responsibility to make sure that their kids stayed inside the house while being on the house arrest.

JP and I could no longer stay with Lisa anymore because of the house arrest; we were forced to go back to our parent's house but that was the last place that we wanted to go back to.

After my father hit me in the head with that broom I never planned on going back there ever again! Also I didn't need to be reminded of the terrible thing that my mother forced me to do!

Meantime, Lisa was throwing a party and I really wanted to go but I knew I couldn't; for some reason my parents weren't home and I decided to sneak out of the house regardless of me being on the house arrest; I caught the bus to the party anyway.

By the time I arrived the party was jumping; everyone was enjoying themselves and having mass fun. Lisa had this big wooden box that we called "the stage"; this box was big enough for at least five or six people to stand on and dance. People were dancing on the stage; others were going down a soul train line.

The bathtub was filled with ice and plenty of beer and wine coolers; I was having the time of my life until somehow my mother found out that I was at the party; soon my fun was about to end.

My mother called Lisa and told her to send me home A.S.A.P; I told Lisa that I wasn't ready to go home yet because I'd just got there and it was no way that I was leaving that soon.

However, my mother called again and said that she was on her way to get me; I continued to party until she arrived and that's when I decided to run into the bathroom and lock myself inside.

People started pounding on the door; they wanted to use the bathroom or get something to drink. However, I wasn't opening up that door until the coast was clear. Although I wasn't planning on coming out the bathroom, my mother was planning on coming in.

She got a screwdriver and started taking the screws out of the bathroom door. After she got inside she dragged me out in front of everybody at that party. I was so embarrassed and humiliated that I was too ashamed to show my face anymore!

However, my mother didn't believe in beatings but she did throw a mean punch; she only had to punch me one good time in my back and that was enough to knock the wind out of me!

Meanwhile, after getting off the house arrest I decided to hang around my parent's house. I stayed back and forth between both my parent's house and my sister's place; I had two resident.

My hormones were really messed up from taking all those pills and my menstrual cycle was really off. Sometimes I would have periods for thirty days straight nonstop and I use to think that I was going to bleed to death! I was always constantly bleeding!

Not only were my hormones all screwed up so were my emotions! I still had this big void that lived deep inside of me and I still thought I needed to fill that void by getting pregnant again!

—∘∘○)●(○∘∘—

Meantime, I turned sweet sixteen... However, there wasn't anything sweet about it! I often thought about my baby that I'd destroyed and I felt really depressed. I also thought about how Lackey destroyed my relationship with Walden! As far as Tony was concerned I still can't remember what happened between us!

Anyhow, somehow I thought if I could see Walden one more time that maybe it would help ease my depression. I asked Pamela Jean if she would go with me to help me find his house.

However, there was a curfew in effect and no one could be on the streets after a certain hour; Pamela Jean and I ended up sneaking out of the house and we found a party in Walden's neighborhood; somehow we ended up going to the party instead.

That night we met these two guys and decided to hang out with them. Since we couldn't be out on the streets I suggested we go over Lisa place; she was at our parent's house but that night somehow I just so happened to have the door keys to her place!

However, at the time there wasn't any electricity in her apartment but we still hung out there and had conversation and got high. I hooked up with a guy named Daryl and my plan was to get involved with him and somehow try to get pregnant by him!

Our relationship lasted until he left town for a job that was in Washington DC; however I didn't get pregnant before he left. Later in life I heard that he came back to Ohio and somehow he ended up dying at the hands of the police. What a shame!

Meanwhile, I still wanted to become pregnant so bad that I got involved with this guy named Mannie; he lived in the same building as one of JP's sisters and we ended up having a very short relationship. Speaking of short was the reasons why our relationship didn't last very long.

Somehow even when I wore flat shoes he was still a lot shorter than me! I felt really self-conscious whenever we were seen in public! Somehow I let his height get in the way of a really good relationship! This was so shallow and very immature of me!

Meantime, Connie and I dressed alike wearing our little sizzler outfits with the matching panties and hung out in this local bar called the Clock-Bar. One day my sister Bev busted us in that bar and told our parents on us; we both were put on punishment.

After Connie and I got off punishment we decided to hang in another local bar with Pamela Jean. We met this older man in his late sixties and he was sloppy drunk. He offered us money to have sex with him and later we ended up going to his house!

Little did the old man know we had other intentions in mind; we needed the money but wasn't willing to have sex with him; our plan was to trick him and get whatever we could get out of him.

Pamela Jean got the old man into his bed and took off all of his clothes and tied him to his bed; Connie and I went through his house and looked for whatever valuables that we could find.

After gathering a few things we decided to unscrew all the light bulbs and hid them in his oven; we needed for his house to be pitch dark before making our grand escape. However, I don't know what possessed us to do something that stupid...?

After putting all of the light bulbs inside the oven we told Pamela Jean it was time to get the hell up out of there. As we ran out the door we heard all this loud popping noises! At first we thought the old man had gotten a loose and was shooting at us!

Connie told us after we put all of the light bulbs inside the stove that she turned the oven on. The loud popping noises that we heard were all those light bulbs exploding inside the oven!

After getting outside we ran as fast as we could; we thought maybe somehow the old was following behind us! We decided to take a shortcut and started cutting through people's backyards.

Somehow, Pamela Jean fell and broke both heels off of her shoes; she ended up rolling down someone's driveway and knocked over their garbage cans; it made a loud crashing noise!

However, she must have woke up the whole neighborhood because everybody started turning on their lights and looking out their windows; we thought the old man had called the cops on us!

After we finally got home we told Ronnie about our little adventure; he wanted in on the stuff that we'd taken. "He said if we didn't give him anything he'd tell on us what we had done".

We told him that he wasn't getting nothing! Little did we know that he had a trick up his sleeve for us; after a few days passed he decided to pay us back for not giving him anything.

He called our houses and disguised his voice and pretended to be a police officer named Sergeant O'miley; he said that they were investigating a robbery and the police had our finger prints.

However, we had no idea that it was really Ronnie on the phone; we thought it was really the police and we were in serious trouble! He really had us going and let us sweat for a couple of days before revealing it was really him. Ha-ha Ronnie very funny!

Meantime, it became harder for Connie to get a baby sitter; for some reason her mother stopped watching her baby; therefore she couldn't always hang out with us whenever she wanted to!

However, I was still trying to find someone special in my life to help me fulfill my hopes in becoming pregnant again; however, somehow it didn't seem like I was having much luck in that matter.

One day on my way over Pamela Jean's house I met this guy named Richard. He asked if I get two of my girlfriends and hang out with him and his two friends. Although he wasn't my cup of tea I told him sure why not; what the hell; I was so bored.

I ended up getting Pamela Jean and JP and we hung out with Richard and his two friends; we smoked weed and got drunk with them. Since I was the first one to meet Richard somehow I ended up getting stuck sitting in the front seat next to him.

Pamela Jean hooked up with his friend named Teddy and JP hooked up with his other friend named Jimmy. As the night went on I realized that I didn't have anything in common with Richard.

However, I had my eyes on the guy that JP was with; he was this really cute guy and I thought maybe I could get pregnant by him. Richard was getting so obnoxious; he was on my last nerve!

I didn't know how much more that I could take being with him; the situation between us got so bad that we got into this big argument; it almost led us into getting into a physical altercation!

Later that night, we took Teddy to get his car so that he and Pamela Jean could follow behind us. We ended up going over another one of their friends house to drink and smoke some more.

While we were at their friend's house I told JP that I couldn't deal with Richard anymore! I asked if she'd switch guys with me; she said yes because she wasn't into Jimmy but it was no way that she'd be with Richard after seeing how obnoxious he was.

I asked her if I'd arranged for her to be with the guy that Pamela Jean was with would she switch places with her instead. However, this would cause Pamela Jean to end up with Richard and allow me to hook up with the guy that JP was with.

JP said "she had no problem being with the guy that Pamela Jean was with just as long as she didn't end up with Richard"; so I came up with this big plan and it was time for the switch to begin.

After we left out of their friend's house JP went towards the car with the guy that Pamela Jean was with. I told Jimmy to join me in the backseat of Richard's car. However, that left Pamela Jean to sit in the front seat next to Richard's annoying ass!

Pamela Jean didn't know what was going on or how she ended up with him. She was mad at us for pulling a fast one on her but it was better her being with him then me being with him.

Although I'd just met Jimmy I was still in the backseat trying to make a baby with him. I was so desperate to get pregnant that I didn't care that I didn't know nothing about him other than the fact that he was so cute; but that night ended up becoming really ugly!

Somehow, Pamela Jean was in the front seat breaking beer bottles trying to cut Richard; she kept yelling "hit me you no-good for nothing mother fucker; I will kill you, you crazy ass bastard".

JP and Teddy were still following behind us; they didn't know what was going on inside of Richard's car. They said "all they saw was legs up in the air and bottles flying around the car".

I really tried getting it on with Jimmy but Richard and Pamela Jean threw a wrench in my plans; or shall I say threw a bottle! With all the glass that was flying around in the car made it impossible to have sex! Therefore I didn't get pregnant that night.

JP was such a good friend and she didn't even mind switching guys with me; that's just how close we were! However, that's what makes it so hard for me to understand the reason why I never mention anything about Tony to her...? I do wonder why!

Meanwhile, one day while walking home I met this other guy named Lawrence and he offered me a ride home. However, back in those days my friends and I had a bad habit of thumbing rides from people we didn't know; # complete unknown strangers!

Normally I wouldn't get into a car by myself but this day I did; he seemed to be a nice enough guy and I thought that I could trust him; little did I know then this guy had other motives in mind.

He asked if I wanted to hang out with him and I thought that it would be ok; he offered to let me drive his car although I didn't have a driver's license. However, I didn't know that he was setting me up for one of the biggest trick bags that ever was!

Lawrence told me to get on the highway and drive out towards Kings Island. However, after driving for a while he then asked me to pull over so that he could take over the wheel again.

After I pulled his car over he said "give it up or get out!" Lawrence you dirty dog you! Here I was done drove myself out in the middle of nowhere and he tried it! What a low down shame!

I was so distraught that I didn't know what to do next. I didn't want to give it up nor did I want to get out. However, I was just too far away from home so I slowly started unbuttoning my pants!

However, God must have sent help to me that day because at that very moment out of nowhere somehow the state trooper showed up and pulled right behind his car!

When he saw the cop walk towards his car he begged me not to tell on him and promised to take me straight home! Call me stupid, crazy or just plain ole dumb but regardless of what just happened I don't know why but for some reason I trusted him! When the cop asked if everything was alright I didn't say a word. However, Lawrence kept his promise and he drove me straight to my front door; as I exited his car I told him to lose my number!

However, he kept calling me trying to apologize; he had a lot of balls thinking that I would ever talk to him again after he tried to manipulate me into having sex with him; that fool must be crazy!

Meanwhile, I turned seventeen years old...My hormones were still screwed up and I noticed that my depression was getting worse!

I tried not to think about my baby getting flushed down that toilet but in the back of my mind that memory just kept repeating itself over and over again! I just couldn't stop thinking about it!

Meantime at school, my Guidance Counselor helped me get into a program called O.W.E.; this program allowed me to go to school for a half of day and work the other half to receive credits. I landed a job as a nurse's aide working at Veteran's Hospital.

Being able to get credits for working plus get paid I couldn't ask for anything more! Also another good thing about the program was I could still leave school early even on my days off. This was a win, win situation. The O.W.E program was the best thing ever!

I took up a journalism class and somehow being in that class really helped me keep my mind off the dreadful thing that my mother forced me to do! I was appointment the staff artist for our school's newspaper called the Gargoyle; my teacher encouraged me to write articles for the paper along with being the staff artist.

After I graduated my teacher wanted me to pursue a career in writing or in the news field as a reporter. If only I'd took her up on her advice then maybe my life would have been a lot better off.

Meantime, I met a few of the orderlies at my job at Veteran's hospital. I met this guy named Earney; and another guy named Will who I ended up having a relationship with. Both guys were in their late twenties and much older than me.

Earney tried hooking up with Connie but that didn't work out; so he tried hooking up with me but I wasn't interested. However before Will and I hooked up I do re-call letting Earney finger fuck me once; I guess at that particular time I just needed to get off...?

I also met another guy who called himself Brother Me; he also worked at the hospital as one of the orderlies; he was also much older than me. One day he offered to buy me lunch; I was glad because I was hungry and didn't have any money that day.

However, that next day I saw him wearing a hospital gown; at first I was shocked and didn't know what to think. One day he was an orderly; the next day he's a patient. What the hell...?

I started thinking perhaps he really didn't work at the hospital and maybe he was just one of the crazy patients pretending to work there. However, he later explained that he'd signed his self in the hospital because he was going through a deep depression that required immediate medical attention!

Brother Me served in the army in Nam as a Vietnam Veteran who suffered from being shell-shocked. He wanted to leave the hospital but for some reason they wouldn't sign his release papers! He asked if I'd returned his favor for him buying my lunch that day. However, his favor was for me to help him escape!

He asked if I knew how to drive and gave me the keys to his car; he wanted me to bring it around to the front of the hospital. Since he was nice enough to buy me lunch that day I went ahead and got his car for him so that he could leave the hospital.

Just so happens he lived right down the street from Lisa's so he offered me a ride home. After my sister took one good look at him she didn't know what to think about him by him only wearing just a hospital gown; but she was tripping very hard off of him.

Meanwhile, my other sister Tonya divorced her husband and moved from the church and moved into a building called the Alms; it had a night club downstairs; my friends and I often party there.

Will and I started hanging at Tonya's new place; he was almost the perfect guy to get me pregnant but somehow he had one serious drinking problem; # he loved him some wine!

I remember drinking Wild Irish Rose, Thunderbird and MD 20-20 with him; sometimes he'd get so drunk that he'd pass out anywhere! He was definitely a wine head and couldn't go a day without having some wine in his system!

Meantime, I made a shocking discovery concerning him; it's when he invited me to his place for my very first time. Little did I know then it was a reason why he never invited me there before!

It all happened one day right after he and I just got finished making love and I heard somebody come through his front door downstairs; for some reason he didn't seem too surprised about it.

We were upstairs in his bedroom when I asked him who was coming in his front door; he replied it was his wife! "Wife" I said; what wife...? I knew nothing about any wives. # OMG!

Before I could say anything else all of a sudden two little girls came running up the stairs. I was still laying there butt naked with only a sheet covering my body; suddenly these two little girls came running into the bedroom and yelling for their daddy!

At that point I remember I just froze up; I wanted to get up and put my clothes on but somehow I couldn't move! Then the two little girls started asking daddy, daddy who is this women...?

Right as Will was about to answer them his wife came into the room. By that time I was still too afraid to get up so I just laid there still butt naked and frozen with fear.

At that very moment all kinds of craziness was running through my head; I was thinking that this woman was about to pull a gun out and shoot me in the head for being with her husband.

However, she told the kids to wait downstairs and she started slamming the dresser drawers and throwing clothes out of the closet. She and Will went into another room and I heard them arguing and cussing at each another.

I didn't know what was going to happen next but I started thinking that I didn't want to die in that bed naked so I hurried up and put my clothes back on!

However, I found it to be really strange that Will never bothered to mention anything about having a wife or any children; later he explained that he was in the process of getting a divorce!

However, after finding out about his family the way that I did our relationship went downhill. It bothered me that he didn't tell me up front about them! After that and along with his drinking problem it all became a little bit too much to deal with; # it's over!

Meanwhile, the need to get pregnant was still a number one priority; I was still grieving the loss of the baby that I'd destroyed. Weed and alcohol wasn't enough anymore to cover up the pain that I was still feeling inside! I took these pills called Thorazine*.

Somehow, I thought that I could take six pills all at once; that was a very big mistake! However, after taking all six pills I passed out and didn't remember what happened after that.

That next day Earney came over to visit JP and I remember waking up and trying to get in the room with them. The door must have been locked because I remember struggling to get inside. Once I got in I dove in between them and passed right back out.

For some reason I just needed to be near someone; little did I know that I had overdosed off those pills! However, no one bothered to take me to the hospital to get my stomach pumped.

Somehow, I slept for a total of three days; when I woke up I was very thirsty and very hungry. I couldn't believe that I'd slept for those three days; I just thank God that I didn't die in my sleep!

Meantime, I stayed high every chance I could. One day some guy that lived in my sister's building asked JP and I if we wanted to get high off some weed laced with embalming fluid; we decided to try it somehow. After smoking it; it gave me a feeling that I never felt before! I felt like I was floating on a cloud.

It was almost like I didn't exist anymore! However, smoking the weed laced with the embalming fluid helped take away the sadness that lived deep within my soul. I felt so numb inside and somehow nothing seemed to matter anymore; # I was carefree!

One of my sister's friends and her daughter were also at this guy's house and her daughter was around four or five years old; she was the type of child that got into anything and everything!

I remember that day seeing her eating some comet that contained bleach; we told her mother but she didn't seem too concerned about it. We continued smoking the laced weed but the more we smoked it was the more that reality started fading away!

The guy that gave us the embalming fluid tried to convince us that the child was really possessed by the devil. He said "the reason why the comet didn't have any effects on her was because she was evil and spawned by Satan". However, everything started becoming harder to distinguish what was real and what wasn't.

We were so high and messed up off that shit that we didn't realize just how crazy that guy really was! He told us "he was going to prove to us that her daughter was really possessed".

He took a pair of ladies panty hose and tied them around the child's waist and hung her out the ninth floor window! He said "if she didn't fall that it meant that she was really possessed by the devil". JP and I both thought that he was going to kill her; we started screaming for him to bring her back inside immediately!

We may have been high out of our damn minds but we had sense enough to know that if that stocking would have broken that she would have fallen to her death! We were able to convince that crazy ass lunatic to bring her back inside before it was too late!

One thing that I learned about doing drugs is you have to do the drug and don't let the drug do you!!! Make sure that whatever situation you get in always be in control at all times! Never let the drug control you no matter what! Keep a strong mind and always put your mind over the matter! Better yet try not to do drugs at all.

Meanwhile, my sister moved into another building that JP's brother-in-law sometimes hung out at; he and I became the King and Queen of mastering the dance called the Scorpio and both of us just so happen to be born under the zodiac sign "Scorpio".

However, we ended up doing more than just the dance together; somehow we had sex but it was just a booty-call. However, this didn't affect my friendship with JP in any way!

I'm so glad that JP didn't tell her sister about me sleeping with her husband; I'm also glad I didn't get pregnant by him! If I would have gotten pregnant it would have been a big disaster!

Meanwhile, my sister Lisa gave birth to her third child; my niece Marla was born. I got involved with some guy that lived in Lisa's neighborhood that called himself Corkey.

Our relationship started off good and I thought that he would be the one to get me pregnant; however, his zodiac sign was "Libra" and sometimes our personalities clashed.

One day, we got into this big argument over my class ring because I asked for it back and he threw a glass of tea in my face! However, I think he gave my ring to one of his side chicks.

Later, I did find out that he was cheating on me but the sad part about it was how I found out. I got a phone call from the Health Department saying that someone turned my name in and they needed for me to come in right away and get tested.

I was so scared and didn't know what was going on. I told my sister that I wasn't going to the Health Department and she explained that if I didn't go they'd send a car to pick me up; somebody that I had sex with had a sexually transmitted disease!

However, the only person that I had sex with was Corkey. Before I made it to the Health Dept. I started itching down in my private area and that's when I saw all these little bugs crawling.

Oh no he didn't …Not only did he give me gonorrhea; his dirty ass gave me crabs too. What kind of low down, dirty ass, tramp, hoe, was he messing with…? Probably the same slut that he gave my class ring to; it ain't no tellin!

Meanwhile, Connie's family was planning this New Year's Eve party and her older brother Bo asked me if I'd go with him to his apartment to help him gather a few things for the party.

At that time I didn't think much about it; besides Bo never gave me no reason not to trust him! His apartment was just right around the corner from his parent's house so I decided to go.

After we arrived we smoked some weed and then he asked me if he could have oral sex with me. I was so shocked he asked me something like that; I didn't see that coming! I was blindsided.

However, I knew nothing about oral sex then and didn't want to know about it. My hormones were still all screwed up and I was on my period bleeding really heavy that day. The thought of someone wanting to eat my bloody pussy was a real live turn off.

Bo started drinking whiskey and kept on begging me to let him eat my pussy. I told him I was bleeding hoping that would somehow discourage him from wanting to do something like that.

However, I was wrong; somehow he didn't care and still wanted to eat me! Oh hell no; it was no way I was going to let him do something that gross; but for some reason he wasn't taking no for an answer and he kept trying to pursue me with the matter!

He tried to force himself on me and somehow we got into this big scuffle; I started picking up all kinds of stuff and started throwing things at him trying to stop him from overpowering me!

He almost succeeded in getting my pants off but somehow I fought him off with all my might; I was determined not to let him take advantage of me! I'd rather died that day than to have let him go down on me! Just the thought of it was too damn gross!

However, somehow he finally got tired of fighting with me and somehow he just gave up. I was so grossed out afterwards that I ended up throwing up all over his living room floor.

On our way back to his parent's house Bo just kept trying to apologize to me; he begged me not to say anything to anybody. Before I got out of his car he gave me four-hundred dollars and an ounce of weed; I guess that was supposed to be hush money!

However, I was too embarrassed and too ashamed to tell anybody anyway! I didn't even tell his sister; my best friend Connie and I told her everything! Later that night we smoked the weed and I put what her brother tried to do to me behind me!

Meanwhile, my parents moved to another neighborhood. However, I didn't know anybody that lived there but I did meet this guy named Jeff and he showed me around the neighborhood. Jeff was like the brother that I never had but always wanted.

One night, JP, Jeff and I and a friend of his were all sitting in Jeff's car getting high; it was one of those days that JP and I were both very depressed. We started saying things like we wished that we were dead and thought about possibly committing suicide!

Jeff's car was parked on this really steep hill and out of no-where the car started rolling slowly down the hill; Jeff immediately put his emergency brakes on and luckily the car stopped rolling.

As JP and I continued having our conversation about wishing that we were dead; all of the sudden the car started rolling again! However, this time it was rolling extremely fast.

At that very moment, I saw my whole life flash before my eyes; it was as if God heard us talking that night and was testing us! JP and I yelled out "please God we don't really want to die"!

Somehow the car crashed into a tree and suddenly it just stopped. I thank God that no one was hurt! As the ole saying goes... Be careful what you wish for because you never know; somehow your wish could come true; # so be really careful ok.

Meantime, my niece Robin came to live with my parents. My family became close friends with a couple of their neighbors; a lady named Elonora and her husband Leon and their kids Chris, Tradewind, Nikki and Man all became lifelong friends of my family. Other kids in the neighborhood were Pookie, Tee, Kim, Daimen, and GG; they too became lifelong friends of the family.

I also became close friends with a girl named Jackie; she lived a few doors down from my parent's house. She introduced me to a few people in the neighborhood and one of them had this Ouija board. They asked if I wanted to play with it but I never played with an Ouija board before. I was curious to find out how it worked so they told me to ask the board any yes or no question.

I asked the board whether or not if I would ever become pregnant again...? Somehow the board started off by spelling out the word Y-E-S; however, at first I thought that maybe Jackie or somebody else was making the board move!

However, she and everyone else swore that they weren't making the board move and somehow it was moving by itself. I then asked it something else that wasn't a yes or no question; I asked the board if my child would be a boy or a girl...? However, somehow the Ouija board then spelled out the letters G-I-R-L.

At that moment I started freaking out; it was my very first time ever experiencing anything like that before! Little did I know then that in my future I'd somehow end up having a baby girl!!

Meanwhile, Brother Me was planning a trip to South Carolina to visit his mother; he asked Connie, Sade and I if we wanted to ride along with him on the trip.

I always wanted to travel so I was excited for the opportunity and was really looking forward to going on the trip. Connie and Sade already turned eighteen years old; I was still just seventeen.

Brother Me said we were coming right back and we didn't need to pack anything. I remember the "Love Unlimited" theme song was playing in his car as we road down the highway.

When we traveled through Atlanta we stopped at a gas station to gas up and get something to eat. I remember standing on this street corner and feeling this rumbling underneath our feet.

That day something shook the ground really hard; at first we thought it was a bunch of bikers riding by or a big truck passing by; however, I think it may have been a small earthquake...?

Anyway when we got to Augusta Georgia Brother Me told us to call our parents to let them know that we were alright. However, I never bothered telling my parents that I was leaving town; they had no idea that I was even gone out of Cincinnati.

When I called my mother she told me that I had one hour to return home! One hour and I was all the way in Augusta Georgia; really mother are you serious...? It's no way; # mother be for-real.

My mother was so mad at me that she threaten to send me away and get Brother Me in trouble for taking a minor out of town. Somehow I didn't let her threats bother me and we continued to our destination to South Carolina.

When we first arrived in South Carolina something came up concerning his mother; this caused us to stay longer then we planned and Brother Me ended up getting us a hotel room.

That next morning he took Connie to buy us some personal items including an outfit and shoes to change into. However, I knew when it came time to head back home I was going to be in some really big trouble; I knew my ass was out for leaving town.

I wore the outfit home that Brother Me picked out for me; it was this long, orange and white dress that looked like some kind of prom dress along with some white high heeled shoes that were two sizes too big for me. I'll never forget how ridiculous I looked.

I had Brother Me drop me off down the street from my parent's house when I first got back; I didn't want my mother seeing him. I was too afraid that she might call the police on him!

I remember as I walked towards my parent's house how afraid I was to face my mother; I didn't know what she might do to me or what she had planned on doing to Brother Me.

When I first walked into the house I saw the anger in my mother's eyes. However, after she took one good look at me she busted out laughing at how ridiculous I looked in that outfit.

However, it was that outfit that kept my mother from going off on me! Thank goodness for that long, ugly, orange dress and those big ole white shoes; somehow that outfit saved my ass!

I found out while we were gone that my mother teamed up with Brother Me's wife and they planned on putting him behind bars; somehow their little plan failed and it never happen!

Meanwhile, once again JP and I decided to stay with Lisa again; I'll never forget the day when we knocked on her door. I bet you won't guess who answered it...? Oh my God it was Lackey; the same man that destroyed my very first relationship I ever had!

JP and I were so shocked we couldn't believe our eyes after he answered Lisa's door; we thought we were seeing things. I said to myself how could this even be possible...? Out of all the people in the world how was it Lackey that answered her door...?

However, he had the nerve to ask us why we were knocking on her door. Wait a minute now; I should be the one asking all the questions! Lackey was in my sister's house! He explained that his best friend said that he could stay there temporary. Say what...

At that time Lisa's boyfriend Anthony lived with her and somehow Lackey was his best friend. Lackey was having problems with his baby's momma so Anthony asked my sister if his best friend could stay there until he sorted things out.

At that time neither Lisa nor Anthony was at home; this was my first time seeing Lackey since I was fifteen at the club! I guess it was meant to be...? However, seeing him again it somehow opened up Pandora's Box and I knew I was in serious trouble!

Meantime, by him staying at my sister's place I could get with him anytime I wanted too. Only this time our relationship wasn't like it was before at age fifteen; this time it became sexual.

There weren't any more excuses why we couldn't finally be together; at least that's what I thought. However, Lackey was this great master mind of manipulation; he knew just how to play me!

I was still so desperate to fulfill my hopes on becoming pregnant again I became highly influence by all of his sexual desires! However, I found out that the whole time that we were having sex he was also having sex with Anthony's younger sister.

Lackey was then almost twenty-three years old; he was still quite the ladies' man; he was still messing around with women in every community. I guess you can say that he was a male whore!

Meanwhile, he moved out of my sister's apartment and went back to his baby's momma; they already had a couple of kids together and her kids were the only kids he claimed; he didn't claim any of his other kids that he had scattered all over town!

Meanwhile, Lisa became friends with a lady down the hall from her named Bernice; she had a sister that was around my age named Deb and somehow we became life-long friends.

Another friend who I met and became life-long friends with was a home girl named Lena; together we developed this ride or die type of relationship! When it came down to dealing with any men drama we were always scheming on how to handle it.

Also in the building was a lady named Carmen; after she moved out her ex-boyfriend Elbert took over her apartment and I remember him having these wild orgies; he often tried getting me to join in on one of them but I told him sorry I didn't do the dozens!

Meanwhile, I turned eighteen years old... By then I just knew that I was grown. I was a couple of credits short from graduating so I decided to enroll in night school to get the credits that I needed.

My sister Bev gave birth to her second child; my niece Erica was born. It seemed like every time that someone in my family got pregnant or gave birth it caused me to somehow go right back into a deep depression! I wanted to be the one getting pregnant!

However, I started popping all kinds of different pills; I tried uppers, downers, Reds, Black Mollies, Opie's and something called Angel dust and Window pane; I also smoked some Hash.

The only drug that I wouldn't try was heroin but I did snort cocaine. However, I truly believe that sniffing cocaine up my nose somehow caused me to later on developed sinus problems!

Meantime, Brother Me had some sort of flashback that led him to believe that he was back in the Vietnamese War. It all started when these people down the hall from Lisa started messing with her for no reason; probably because of jealousy!

Brother Me asked these people to leave her alone; however, they kept on saying all kinds of crazy stuff to her; this provoked him to go after these people! This was the first time that I ever seen him in that state of mind; Brother Me was O.O.C.

He kept saying if those people didn't shut up and leave Lisa alone that he was going to drive his car through their window. Everyone kept telling me to talk to him; they thought I could be his voice of reasoning and talk him out of doing something crazy!

However that night Brother Me was in some sort of zone; there was no reasoning with him! No matter whatever I tried to say he was still determined to drive his car into their window!

It was a big storm outside that night and it was pouring down rain and thunder and lightning. I remember being barefoot and running through the mud trying to stop him; I felt like I was in somebodies war getting ready for a battle in the combat zone!

There was no stopping him and somehow he ended up crashing his car inside their window anyway! I thought once he crashed his car that all the drama was finally over but it wasn't...

He came back inside Lisa's house and grabbed this big ole machete and headed for the people's door; I was too afraid to know what he was going to do next. Lord please help him!

He knocked on their door and some dude stuck his arm out. All of the sudden he took that big ole machete and cut the man's hand half way off. Oh my God; I couldn't believe that he did that.

When the police showed up they didn't take Brother Me to jail due to his mental state of mind; instead he was taken to the VA hospital. He was really messed up and needed serious help!

However, the dude was taken to the hospital to have his hand sewed back on; later I heard that Brother Me paid him off not to press any charges on him for almost cutting his hand off.

Meantime, Lackey wasn't giving up on me; for some reason he continued to come around Lisa's place. However, I don't know what allowed me to keep letting this man come back into my life!

I guess perhaps in my heart I still felt that he owed me for destroying my relationship with Walden; or maybe it was his charming manipulative ways! Perhaps it was because he was such a damn good lover; but whatever the case may have been somehow he definitely had some sort of hold on me!

Meanwhile one day, Deb, JP, Sade and I were all minding our own business looking for something to get into. Along came this little red car with this very unusual, crazy sounding horn.

However, that crazy horn captured our attention and we all went over to the car and introduce ourselves to these four guys. The driver's name was Bob; his other three friends were, JB, Rick and David; they asked if we wanted to hang out with them.

The car was very small but we all said yes and managed to piled in by sitting on top of their laps; I couldn't believe that all eight of us fitted in that little biddy car but somehow we all did.

The fellows had some weed and we all went across the bridge to Kentucky to a liquor store to get a bottle; then we went to this park called Eden Park so we could hang out and get high.

While at the park we all decided to take a walk on one of the trails; this was the point when everyone started to pair up with each other. I immediately hooked up with the guy named David.

David was this chocolate cutie with a head full of hair and I developed an instant attraction for him! For some reason I just knew that he was somehow going to become my baby daddy.

Sade hooked up with the guy named JB and Deb got with the guy named Rick; that left JP to hook up with the driver Bob.

That night David and I got to know each other and there was definitely some strong chemistry between us! However, Sade and I were the only ones that made a love connection that night!

Meantime, even after that night was over we all continued to be friends and still hung out together. One night we all went to this cemetery to get high. JP and I thought that it would be fun to play like we were witches and give the guys something to talk about. It was time for the mind games to begin; # let's have some fun!

We started fooling around and pretending like we were summoning the dead. We must have really put on a good show because we had them going; they didn't know what to think of us!

Meanwhile, my relationship with David grew stronger by the day and we were deeply in love! We started going out without the rest of the gang being present; it felt really good being able to pull him away from his buddies! David zodiac sign was "Pisces".

Meantime, Sade ended up getting pregnant by JB; they had a daughter named Shannon. I wanted to get pregnant so bad that I was hoping and praying that David would get me pregnant too.

Shortly after Sade had her baby she and I went out to look for a job. We thought about getting a job in Kentucky as one of the dancers at this strip club called the "Foxy Lady".

The club was hiring topless dancers and the job paid very well. Some guy that was high as a kite gave us a ride to the club and he ended up coming inside to watch us try out for the job.

We took center stage and started dropping it like it was hot! Things were going great and the owner of the club was very impressed with our dancing; somehow she wanted to hire us!

However, all of the sudden the guy that took us to the club got his high ass up on the stage and started dancing with us. I thought to myself…Oh no he didn't…Where they do that at…?

The owner asked the guy to remove himself but he just kept dancing all over the place. After being told three times to get off the stage they called security and had him escorted out the club.

Unfortunately that day he was our only ride home so we had to leave out with him. However, we didn't get the job thanks to ole boy for ruining our chances and we were very pissed off about it.

Meanwhile, my sister Lisa and I had some sort of falling out and JP and I decided to leave her apartment but neither one of us wanted to go back to our parent's house!

During that time Brother Me had his own apartment because he and his wife had split up and he offered JP and I a place to stay; he said we could stay with him and we accepted his offer.

However, Brother Me must have somehow flipped out again; I don't know what happened but one day after we left out and upon our return we saw all this stuff lying all over the ground outside! As we got closer to his apartment building we discovered that the stuff lying on the ground was somehow all of our stuff.

For some reason Brother Me had threw out all of our things; it was so embarrassing picking up all of our bras and panties off that dirty ground; people were looking at us like we were crazy!

After gathering all of our belongings we went to see why he threw out our things. However, when we tried to unlock the door he'd already changed the locks; we knocked but he didn't answer.

Later we found out that he had taken a hand full of Valium's and was in the apartment passed out; he was going through another one of his depression spells that caused him to do that.

However, after that crazy messed up incident JP and I didn't have nowhere else to stay. We refused to go back to our parent's house so we ended up homeless and sleeping on park benches!

Meanwhile, Lisa and I put all of our differences aside and made up from whatever stupid reason that we fell out about. After we patched things up I started back staying with her once again.

Meantime, at night school I only had one final test to take on drugs and that would have completed my time and gave me the couple of credits that I needed in order to graduate! However, during that time somehow I ended up getting hooked on Valiums!

Somehow by me taking those Valiums it caused me to drop out of night school; therefore I didn't take that final test and unfortunately I didn't graduate with the rest of my classmates! # ☹

Meanwhile, Brother Me talked me into enrolling in a nursing school. As far as David was concerned things were still great between us! We were madly in love with one another and he was the first guy who I encounter having oral sex with.

However, after that horrible experience I had with Bo I never thought I'd be able to have any parts of having oral sex with anyone but somehow David changed my mind; he was special.

Nothing could come between us at least that's what I thought; until Lackey kept coming back and trying to wreak more havoc on my life! Oh boy here we go again…Lord help me!

Although I was madly in love with David somehow I just kept on having sex with Lackey! I should have known that I was going to be in serious trouble the day he answered my sister's door!

Meanwhile, my best friend Connie got a job at a hospital and she moved into her own apartment. I tried moving forward with only David and I wanted to marry him and have his children but somehow Lackey continued to stay hot on my heels; # stalker!

I tried my best to avoid him because I didn't want him destroying another good relationship again! I stopped answering his calls and refused to see him anymore. One day I went as far as climbing over a big fence just to avoid him from seeing me!

I did everything possible to stay away from Lackey but for some reason I just couldn't; I just kept having sex with him and one day he asked me why didn't I tell him that I was on my period.

However, that's just how messed up my hormones were! I wasn't even aware that I was on that day. I didn't even know what he was talking about until I saw the blood on his boxers myself.

When I talked to my mother she suggested that I go to the doctor to see why I was spotting in between periods. However, by her forcing me to take all those Humphrey's Eleven's was the reason why my hormones were messed up in the first place!

Meantime, I went to the doctor and had a pregnancy test taken; it came back negative and the doctor put me on birth control pills to help regulate my cycle! I took those pills for at least a month but somehow I still continued to spot blood anyhow!

Meanwhile, due to my medical situation it caused me to end up dropping out of nursing school. When I went back to the doctor for a follow-up he decided to give me another pregnancy test.

Only this time the pregnancy test was done through drawing my blood and not like the first test that was done through taking a urine sample and somehow that test showed negative!

However, after testing my blood the doctor came back and said "it showed positive and I was definitely pregnant"...Say what. I've been trying to conceive a baby ever since my mother forced me to abort Tony's unborn child; finally my wish was coming true!

However, I should have been happy and jumping for joy but I wasn't. Instead I was more concerned about who my baby's daddy was...? Was it David or Lackey...? The only way to be 100%sure is to go on the Maury show for D-N-A testing! # ☹

However, my biggest concerned that really had me worried was the fact that I was already pregnant when the doctor had me taking those birth control pills for almost a month! How was that going to affect my unborn child...? I was fearful thinking about it!

Meanwhile, somehow Lackey was involved in something that landed him in serious trouble with the law; he ended up catching a case and was facing five to fifteen years in the penitentiary!

I decided to write David a letter after Lackey got locked up. In my letter I was very truthful; I told him that I was pregnant and I wasn't for sure who the baby's father was because I was having sex with both him and Lackey at the same time!

I remember David telling me when they were in high school that "Lackey had all these girls falling all over him and he must have thought that he was Billy Dee Williams or somebody".

David just couldn't wrap his head around the fact that I wanted somebody like that in my life! He couldn't understand how I got involved with Lackey in the first place; I really couldn't either.

However, after I wrote David that letter somehow our relationship took a wrong turn downhill. Slowly but surely we eventually broke up and I was devastated, pregnant and all alone!

However, this was a bitter sweet moment in my life! On one hand I was finally pregnant; but on the other hand I had no baby's daddy in my life! Lackey was locked up and David was gone out of my life and this wasn't how I planned for my life to turn out.

Meantime, I spent a lot of time at my sister's Bev's house babysitting my niece and nephew. During those times I remember feeling alone and isolated; I found myself in a deep depression!

Elbert's cousin Isadore really helped me during my pregnancy; he took me places that I needed to go and helped me get through my deepest depression. Thanks Isadore...

Meantime, JP was also pregnant with her first child; we spent lots of time together. I decided to go back to my parent's house because I knew my mother would see to it that I ate right and do the things that I was supposed to do while being pregnant.

I wanted to get my own apartment because I knew it was only a matter of time before my mother started getting on my nerves; I went to the welfare for some assistance. I needed help!

However, the apartments that I was trying to get into didn't accept people on welfare. JP knew some dude that owned his own business and he helped me by telling them that I worked for him! Somehow I was able to get into a one bedroom apartment. However, I still stayed at my parent's until I got some furniture.

———∘∘◦}◦{◦∘∘———

Meanwhile, I had my nineteenth birthday... I was still going through a deep depression but looked forward to having my baby! Two months after my birthday my water broke! On January nineteenth, nineteen seventy-six and I went into labor!

Lisa and her boyfriend took me to the hospital and Lavon also came along. I was in so much pain that I started jumping up and down on the bed trying to make the baby fall out of me!

Lavon asked the nurses to give me something for my pain; however, they weren't able to give me anything right then but planned on giving me a spinal tap. I remember my mother saying "when she had me she had a spinal and it messed up her back"!

Before giving me the spinal the doctor said to be real still or it could paralyze me forever; however he didn't bother asking if I was having any contractions before sticking me with that needle!

He just went ahead and stuck me anyway and I ended up jumping as soon as the needle touched my back; all of the nurses and the doctor started yelling at me for making a sudden move!

Later I found out that somehow the movement did cause my spine to shift inwards; just like my mother I too have some back problems from having that spinal. Thank God I wasn't paralyze!

I ended up giving birth to a baby girl weighing five pounds and six ounces; somehow I guess that Ouija board was right after all. Ronnie sent word to the hospital that I better name her after that cat I used to have named Heather and so I did. Her middle name came from the movie "Mahogany" staring Diane Ross.

However, my baby was born premature and she was placed in an incubator; she ended up developing something called yellow jaundice! After I was discharged she had to stay in the hospital. I went home by myself and somehow my depression worsened.

Somehow, I couldn't even find the strength to go visit my baby girl. However, I called and checked on her condition at least ten times a day! I was very concerned about her well-being but not once did I ever go see her in that hospital. # ☹!!!!!!!!!!!!!!!!!!!!

Back then I didn't know anything about any baby blues or postpartum depression! However, I felt worse than I ever felt in my entire life!!! I was in a state of mind that I didn't care whether or not if I lived or died. My depression was off the C-H-A-I-N.....

However, the day my baby was discharged I could barely get out of the bed; I had to dig really deep just to find the strength to go get her. My mother and sister Bev came with me and Bev went upstairs to help me get the baby but my mother waited downstairs because somehow she had this big fear of riding in elevators.

When we first got upstairs the nurses said that "I'd just missed the baby's father; also he left her an outfit to wear home". I was shocked because Lackey was in prison and David was long gone! I had no idea who the nurse was even talking about...?

I was trying to figure out who came to the hospital claiming to be my baby's daddy..? When the nurse described him he fitted David description and I couldn't believe that it was really him!

After we got outside my mother told Bev to carry my baby to the car. However, that pissed me off and I got highly upset. I felt like they were trying to take over. I didn't realize that I only felt that way because of the deep depression that I was going through!

Meanwhile, I stayed at my parent's until I got tired of my mother telling me how to take care of my baby; her constant nagging reminded me of the terrible thing that she forced me to do; so I packed all my things and took my baby to my apartment.

Meantime, I spoke to David and he verified that he was the one who came to the hospital. When I asked him why he told the nurse that he was my baby's father he didn't have any response!

Somehow after having that conversation with him I didn't hear from him again but I did hear from Lackey. He called saying how much he missed me and how much he wanted to see me.

However, there was only one thing wrong with that; Lackey's visitor's list was already filled up and he could only have three visitors; he chose his mother, his brother and his baby's momma.

He came up with a plan to put me on his cellmate's visitors list. Only I wouldn't be visiting his cellmate; I'd be visiting him instead. I wasn't sure if his plan would work but somehow it did.

Lackey would come down in place of his cellmate and somehow the guards didn't know that they'd switched places; this was the point when I started visiting him on a regular basis!

However, for some reason all those times I visited him I never took my daughter to see the man that might be more than likely her father; I would always take my niece instead. I guess deep down I was really hoping that David was my baby's father!

Meantime, whenever I visited Lackey he wanted me to start doing the unspeakable! Call me stupid, crazy, or just plain ole dumb but somehow he convinced me into doing the unspeakable!

However, I was so naïve back then that I didn't think about the consequences or the trouble that I could have been in; even in jail he still had control over me! Somehow he knew how to get his way with me by manipulating me into doing whatever he wanted.

One day I went to visit him and his cell mate came down instead; I was shocked and didn't know what to think. Lackey was transferred to another cellblock so his ex-cellmate wanted me to start visiting him instead.

However, I visited him a few times and wrote him a few letters but then he wanted me to do what I'd done for Lackey! Oh hell no; I wasn't that damn stupid. It was bad enough that I did it for Lackey but it was no way in hell that I'd ever do that again!

Meantime, I stopped writing the cellmate and stopped going to see him; I also stopped writing Lackey as well. I tried putting my past behind me in order to move forward with my future!

I still hadn't heard anything from David and it felt like my life was falling apart. Nothing was going how I planned it to go and I wanted my life to change but I just didn't know how to change it.

Meanwhile, Brother Me offered me and Connie some money to have a threesome. Neither one of us wanted to do it but we really needed the cash! However, after Connie and I started making out somehow we practically forgot all about Brother Me!

Although that was my first time ever becoming sexual with another female; being intimate with Connie didn't make me feel the least bit ashamed or uncomfortable! For some strange reason somehow it felt very natural being with her!

However, I was quite honored to have gotten that chance to become closer than close with her; because little did I know back then that somehow I would soon lose my best friend forever!

Meanwhile, David and I got back together somehow and this time he decided to move in with me! I was finally getting the perfect family that I always wanted and I should have been happy and jumping for joy but for some reason or another I wasn't.

David was this amazing fantastic young man; he accepted my baby not even knowing whether she was his or not. He didn't care because he just wanted our relationship to work out again!

Things were going great between us until I heard news from the great vine; I heard while we were apart that he hooked up with some girl that he was supposed to be totally obsessed over.

I was told that "this girl was the only one that could push David's buttons"; however, I wanted to be the one pushing all his buttons! I started doing really stupid, crazy stuff just to see how far I could go to get underneath his skin; # silly stupid ass me!

I started going out clubbing and leaving my daughter for him to babysit knowing that he had to get up early for work. I'd sometimes come in drunk and high and falling all over the place!

I tried everything to provoke him and push him overboard; however, I always found a way of sabotaging anything good in my life. I don't know why but somehow I was my own worst enemy!!!

Meantime, one morning David and I started arguing over something really stupid and I finally got him to his boiling point. He was so upset that he ended up crashing his car into an apartment building near his mother's house! His car was totaled but thank God he was ok! After that happened he was at his wits end and couldn't take it no more; he had enough of my stupid behavior!

David bent over backwards trying to make me happy but somehow I didn't know how to be happy! Ever since I was forced to kill my own flesh and blood at age fifteen happiness was never an option; I didn't even know the meaning of the word happy!

I'll never forget when he packed all of his things and moved out. The faster he took his things out of the closet was the faster I put them back in. I cried and begged him not to leave me!

I was down on my knees and grabbing his pants leg trying to stop him from leaving me but somehow he left me anyway! I was finally able to succeed in pushing him away all because I acted like a stupid, spoiled, childish, jealous, immature, crazy fool.

When my mother found out about what happened between us she had the nerve to put her two cents in and made some crazy comment by saying that "I didn't want nothing good in my life and that the only thing that I wanted was a no-good thug."

However, my mother only said that based on Walden and the negative opinion of how she felt about him! But what my mother didn't know was that I did want something good alright...

I wanted Tony's baby back that she forced me to get rid of; that would have been good alright. However, I knew that was humanly impossible and I knew that my baby was gone forever!

Meantime, Pamela Jean introduced me to a friend of hers named Cindy; she stayed in the same apartment complex that I lived in and her apartment was right across the walkway from me.

Cindy became Heather's Godmother and also her babysitter; she also became a life-long friend. She was married to a man named Ed and they had a daughter together named Londa.

Some guy named D-Ray also lived in Cindy's building and he had a crush on her. One day he called himself getting mad at me because I told her something about him; he had the nerve to come over my house and tried to whip me with a belt; # funny!

Meanwhile, I turned twenty years old... Little did I know then that things were about to turn tragic really soon. It was four days after Christmas when everything suddenly changed in my life!

Cindy and I planned on going over Connie's that night but somehow we changed our minds and didn't go. I spoke to Connie over the phone to let her know we wouldn't be able to make it but we planned on seeing her that next day after she got off of work.

When the following day came I tried calling Connie but she never answer her phone; I just thought maybe she was working late so I continued trying to reach her throughout the day.

I started to worry about her and later that evening one of her family members called and asked if I've spoken to her. I told them that I'd talked to her the night before but hadn't been able to reach her since then. Connie's mother called her job and they said that she never showed up for work nor did she bother to call in.

However, we all thought it was so strange because she would have never taken off work without calling in; everyone was really concerned because this didn't sound like Connie at all.

Later that evening her mother and her cousin my X Walden decided to go by her apartment to make sure that she was alright. However, the building that she stayed in kept their outside doors locked; no one could get inside without having a key unless she came to let them in herself; the building was very strictly secure.

They rung Connie's doorbell but she never answered her door. Her mother asked the landlord to open up her apartment so that she and Walden could get inside to go check on her.

Once they were inside they noticed that her stereo was missing. When they went into her bedroom they saw Connie lying face down on her bed; at first they thought she was just sleeping!

After touching her body that's when they discovered that she wasn't sleeping; somehow Connie was dead!!! Oh my God… Someone had killed my best friend; she had been strangled by her own telephone cord and it was still wrapped around her neck!

Meantime, there were many details about her death that the news reporters just couldn't release at that time but whoever killed her must have taken their time in doing so.

Somehow a knot was placed in the cord every time it was wrapped around her neck; it was as if it was braided. She had several cigarette burns all over her body including on the inside of her vagina! What sick ass person would do some shit like that…?

Everyone was devastated and wanted to know who had done such a terrible thing to such a sweet, lovely, young lady...? Connie would have turned twenty-one that following month but she never made it to see her twenty-first birthday; ☹ so very sad!

Meantime, I worked with the detective that handed her case. By me being Connie's best friend I knew more about her than anyone else; I was determined to help the detective find her killer.

However, the detective felt that her case was not based on a robbery and the motive seemed to be more personal; they wanted to talk to all her friends and everyone that was involved with her.

Connie had a love interest in a guy named Jessie; however I never thought of him as being a suspect. I just couldn't see him being the murderer; I knew that he wasn't the one that killed her.

However, there was this other guy who I never got a chance to meet; sometimes Connie would mention him but he was just somebody that she kicked it with whenever she got bored.

I remember her telling me that she would let this guy come over sometimes and smoke weed; however, I only knew his first name but the detectives were still very determine to find her killer.

Somehow, Cindy and I felt responsible for her death! We felt that if we'd gone over to her apartment that night liked we planned on going then maybe she'd still be alive right now...?

However, everyone told us maybe it's a good thing that we didn't go over there that night because Cindy and I could have ended up dead too. Well I guess that's something will never know!

Meantime, it came time for Connie's awake and funeral; the killer was still on the loose and everyone was still trying to figure out who murdered her and why...? We all needed answers!

I kept getting this gut feeling that somehow her killer would show up sooner or later; sure enough he had the nerve to show up at her awake! As Connie laid there in her coffin somehow the killer was looking at her dead body but nobody knew it was him!

However, all of her family members and friends were on the lookout looking for anyone that looked suspicious but no one knew that the killer was amongst us!!! Everybody was still talking about her death even after she was buried and somehow her death seemed to be the topic of everyone's conversation!

Meantime, my sister was hanging with friends and usually she would have been talking about her death; however something told her not to say anything around the people that she was with!

Some guy was there that my sister never saw before and he was getting high off of acid and doing other drugs; it's a good thing that my sister didn't mention anything about Connie's death.

Little did my sister know then that the guy who was doing all those drugs was Connie's killer; she was in the company of a maniac and didn't have a clue! I guess you never know whose space you might be sharing; it could be the space of a real killer!

Meantime, as the homicide detectives scrambled to find her killer they contacted me and informed me that a new lead had just turned up; however, this was a major break in Connie's case!!!

Some guy had badly beaten up and raped two other girls; he used a telephone cord to tie them up with. However, by him using that telephone cord somehow it linked him to Connie's case!!!

However, one of the victims name was very similar to my name. At first the detectives thought that it was me who had gotten raped and beat up; he called to make sure that it wasn't me. Luckily one of the victims was able to identify their attacker.

When the police arrested their suspect they discovered a few of Connie's missing items in his possession. There was no doubt about it; finally they had caught Connie's killer! # "Gotcha."

Meantime, her death really took its toll on me; it was very hard for me to accept her death. I felt like shutting down and I became isolated and didn't want to be bothered with anyone!

Connie was the first person that I was close to that died. Her older sister Mary really helped me during this tragic time; she took me to her Church for strength and I spoke in tongue for my very first time! However, if it wasn't for her I don't know what I would have done! I don't think that I would have survived. Thanks Mary!

Meanwhile, her murder trial was beginning and I was summoned to appear in court as a witness for the prosecution. I'd gotten this

Jesus loves you pendant from Mary's Church and I wore that pendant every day during Connie's trial.

However, at the court house there were strange people following me and my friends around; some of them were taking pictures of us and whispering things amongst themselves.

I guess they were the killer's people...? However, my friends and I were very scared; we feared that our lives were in danger. I had to testify against the killer so I myself was especially afraid.

When it was time to take the witness stand the killer's attorney questioned me about some dates; while in the process of questioning me he tried mixing me up by trying to confuse me!

I guess Connie's spirit didn't like that lawyer trying to confuse me! Out of nowhere my Jesus Loves You pendant flew off my blouse and somehow it landed in the very back of that courtroom!

The judge was so stunned that he called for a recess! How that pendant flew that far away still remains a mystery to this very day. However, I think it was definitely Connie in that courtroom!

After the trail was over the killer was sentenced to some years in prison for murdering Connie; he also faced other charges for his other two victims that he'd also beaten up and raped.

Meantime, I was still trying to deal with all the after effects of everything that happened! I just didn't know how I was going to move forward without having my best friend in my life anymore!

Meanwhile, somehow I found out that David had his own apartment and I asked Cindy to babysit while I tried to find him. I thumbed a ride at four o'clock in the morning from some stranger that was leaving out of the parking lot where I lived at.

I must have been really desperate thumbing by myself that time of morning; however, it was a desperate time that called for a desperate measure. I just thank God that my ride wasn't a killer.

After arriving safely at David's house he welcomed me with open arms. I planned on coming right back home but somehow I ended up staying over his house for almost a month.

Cindy kept my daughter the whole time I was gone; I knew that she was in good hands so I wasn't worried about her. I was too busy trying to get her father back into our lives again!

Being with David gave me an ounce of happiness and I didn't want it to end. Unfortunately he'd joined the Navy and he was about to leave town really soon.

Meanwhile, I turned twenty-one years old… Brother Me threw me a surprise birthday party; however, I hated surprises and somehow I found out about the party and decided not to go!

My twenty first birthday party would have been a great big success perhaps if I had showed up. However, I was a no show and the surprise ended up being on everyone else…Sorry y'all!

Meantime, I decided to get my driver's license and become a legal driver; I went all those years driving without a license and it was finally time that I gotten one; it was long overdue!

However, somehow the first time that I took my driving test I failed the parking part; the second time I took the test I borrowed Pamela Jean car with the hatch-back. The instructor let me lift up the hatch and I was able to pass my parking test. Hallelujah!

That same year Sade lost her mother; she passed away and may God bless her mother's soul.

When I turned twenty-two years old… My sister Lisa decided to move close to me within walking distance. However, for some reason she didn't like her new apartment; she decided to let our other sister Tonya stay there while she stayed with me at mines.

One night Tonya babysat for us while Lisa and I went out clubbing. After the club let out Lisa didn't feel like going to get her daughter Marla and wanted to leave her overnight with Tonya.

However, I didn't want to leave my daughter so I planned on going to get her by myself; somehow at the last minute Lisa changed her mind and she decided to come with me.

We told Tonya to have the kids ready when we got there. Lisa parked at the end of the driveway and it was very dark outside; after we gathered the kids we walked towards the car. At first I thought I saw someone coming from behind the building.

I didn't think much about it and we continued to walk towards the car. When I looked back again I saw this guy coming towards us! At first I thought he was some guy we knew that had a beard.

By the time we reached the car this guy was right behind me and that's when I realized that he didn't have a beard on his face; he was wearing a black scarf tied around his face instead!

By then Lisa and Marla had just gotten around to the other side of the car and my daughter was still sound asleep in my arms and somehow this guy was right up on me!

I was able to get inside the car but somehow the guy bum rushed me and tried to get in behind me; that's when I notice that he had a gun in his hand. Somehow I was able to slam the car door on the hand that he was carrying the gun in!!!

I tried to warn Lisa but it all happened so fast; she was still trying to get Marla inside the car. Somehow, this guy managed to get his arm out from the car door and leaped over the top of the car onto the driver's side; he pushed Lisa inside the car and sat down in the driver's seat and pointed the gun in our direction.

We thought that he was trying to rob us so I asked him if he wanted money. He said "shut the fuck up or he'd kill my baby." However, it seemed like he was extra pissed off at me; I guess because I tried to close his arm inside of the car door.

He told us "he just needed a ride downtown and to put our heads down in our laps and don't talk". However, he kept pointing the gun in the backseat at Marla and said "if we raised our heads up that he wouldn't hesitate in blowing her head clean off."

At that point we did what he told us and he started driving for at least fifteen minutes; when he finally stopped the car I knew it was no way that we could have gotten downtown that fast.

However he'd driven us around in circles and we couldn't tell where we were at. He cut the car off and said for us to "keep our heads down or he'd shoot the kids if we didn't do what he said".

Heather was still sound asleep in my arms and Marla was wide awoke in the backseat. I heard the car door open and him telling my sister to get out of the car; then he dragged her out and reminded me that "if I put my head up he'd kill me and the kids"!

After a few minutes passed, I told my niece to look out the back window to see if she could see anything; however, it was too dark outside for her to see anything so I slowly lifted my head up to look out for myself but I couldn't see anything either.

At that moment all I could think about was hearing gun shots go off at any minute; I was really scared for my sister and I didn't have the foggiest idea where he had taken her to. However, it was still dark outside but it was about to turn daylight real soon.

I took off my high heels shoes because I knew I was going to have to run; then I told my niece to slowly climb over to the front seat while I quietly opened up the passenger's side of the door.

I told my niece to grab a hold of my hand and on the count of three to run as fast as she could. However, when I first got out of the car I still didn't know where we were at. All I knew was we were behind a building where there were a lot of trees and woods.

By then it started turning daylight outside and that's when I finally realized where we were at. I was behind a grocery store not far from my apartment but the store was closed. However, I was a little bit surprised that we were still in my own neighborhood.

I ran barefoot with my daughter still sound asleep in my arms and ran to these apartment building that was next door to the store. I tried to get inside but the entrance doors were locked.

Somehow that karate class that I took up when I was younger must have really came in handy; I remember doing a Kun-Fu-kick and breaking out the glass on the door. After I got inside I started banging on people's doors and screaming for help!

It just so happened that a girl that I knew opened up her door; her name was Linda and she was the daughter of the lady that my grandfather once dated. I told her to call the police because I thought that someone may have killed my sister Lisa.

When the cops showed up one of the officers stayed to question me while the other one went outside to look for Lisa. I remember sitting there and thinking that my sister could be dead!

I couldn't just sit there not knowing whether or not if she was still alive; I jumped up and ran outside to the back of the store and that's when I saw the cop and Lisa walking out from the woods.

I just Thank God that she was still alive! However, she had been badly beaten up and raped. The police put her inside the ambulance to receive care and she was taken to the hospital.

Meantime, my sister was going through a really rough period; she became a nervous wreck and was having nightmares! However, both of our nerves were on edge because the rapist was still out there somewhere and he hadn't been captured yet.

Somehow this affected my sister so much that it caused her to go out and buy herself a gun; she took the gun to a shooting range so that she could learn how to shoot it properly!

Meantime one night, me, Lisa and Cindy were coming back from somewhere and Lisa parked her car in my parking lot. Seconds afterwards we heard a loud thump on top of the car.

My sister was so nervous and distraught that she pulled out her gun and was ready to shoot anything in sight. Shoot first and asked questions later is what she was about to do; # bang, bang!

However, it was just a kitty cat that jumped on top of the car; Cindy and I yelled out to Lisa "it's just a cat, don't shoot, don't shoot". Other than that she probably would have shot that cat.

Meanwhile, we received a phone call informing us to come down to the police station for a line up. I wasn't sure if I'd be able to identify the guy because he wore a scarf tied around his face!

However at the police station there were at least twelve other women that had been beaten up and raped on the same night as Lisa. The police told all the women not to discuss anything with anyone about their case or the lineup.

It was hard for us to identify the rapist's since we couldn't see his face; so the police had the men in the lineup say a few words to see if maybe we could somehow recognize his voice!

Later Lisa and I discovered that somehow we'd both picked the same guy from the lineup! Sometimes later we were told all those other women also picked the same guy; however, most of them saw their rapist's face because he wasn't wearing a scarf.

However, I was mentally exhausted and drained from going through all of this. It seemed like I'd just gone through Connie's murder trial and here I was about to face a rape trial. I didn't know how much more I could take; I felt like my life was falling apart.

My depression worsened and I started to feel lonely again; somehow I still had this big void that still lived deep inside of me! My best friend was dead and my sister just got raped! On top of all of that I still had no baby's daddy in my life and that sucked.

Meanwhile, it was time to start lining-up some booty calls. I figured if my heart couldn't find love then my body would. My first booty call was with a young boy who was only eighteen years old.

I started having sex with him until he became too clingy and started getting on my nerves; then I dumped him and had a one night stand with some guy that I knew from my neighborhood.

Meantime, I started messing with this guy who lived in my apartment complex named Russ. However, he was a married man; married to some white girl and they had a couple of kids.

Somehow that booty call ended up becoming more of an affair because it lasted for a good while. He was a stay at home dad and when his wife was at work he'd invite me over his house.

While I was over there Cindy looked after my daughter and Russ sent his kids outside to play. However, after a while I became bored with his sex and I eventually ended our affair.

Meantime, my friends and I would get together and turn-up every night. The manager of my apartment building would put notes on my door complaining about the loud noises that were continually coming from my apartment at all hours of the night.

However, one time something really strange occurred in my apartment. It was when I woke up and found myself lying on the floor by my front door; the cold air is what woke me up! My daughter and I were the only ones in my apartment at the time and my door was still locked with all the chains still on the door.

I woke up lying on the floor without having any panties on. I couldn't figure out how I got on the floor or why I wasn't wearing any panties...? However, I found them hanging on my daughter's baby bed. What a strange place to put them but then again there were a lot of strange things that occurred in that apartment!

However, I came to the conclusion that I must have been sleep-walking again while being horny; I do recall experiencing sleep walking once before when I stayed with my sister Lisa.

I just can't help but to wonder what would have happened if I'd made it outside that door...? I'm just so glad that all those locks and chains stopped me from getting outside that door.

Meantime, there was another strange incident that occur in my apartment; it was one night when a couple of my girlfriends and I got together to turn-up! After they left I started seeing all this strange looking smoke that had a really strange smell; it was so weird and odd; and no it wasn't the smoke from smoking weed.

However at first I thought something was on fire; I tried to find out where this smoke was coming from but I just couldn't seem to figure it out. I saw this big puff of smoke hovering over my head when I went into the bathroom and looked in the mirror!

However, it startled me and I was so frighten that I called my father at 3:00 in the morning to come and get me! My mother answered the phone and said "I probably was just high and tripping and call the fire department"; however, she decided to go ahead and wake my father up and sent him to get me anyway.

By the time he'd arrived the smoke had filled the entire apartment; however, my father didn't come inside to witness this smoke! My apartment would have been burned down if something had been on fire! The next day when I got the nerve to go back in my apartment both my parents went inside with me! However, there was nothing burned or any signs of any kind of smoke!

Then out of nowhere somehow my favorite big tall vase suddenly fell over by its self and broke into a million pieces; however, there was this strange glove inside the bottom of the base and from the looks of it; it had been there for quite a while! I'd never seen this glove before and had no idea how it got there!

However, after my mother witness that vase falling over all by its self for no apparent reason she called over a friend to come and cleanse my apartment of any negative spirits that might be lurking; # other than that I wasn't going to stay there no more!

———∞∘⦿∘∞———

By the time I turned twenty-three years old… One of Lisa's ex-boyfriend told me a rumor that "Lisa slept with Lackey sometimes back when Lackey and I were still together".

Although that happened a long time ago and it was water under the bridge; somehow it still bothered me and I ended up having sex with her X calling myself getting even with her.

This was the same X that was over her house having the candle light dinner the night I left home when my father hit in the head with the broom because I was pregnant with Tony's baby!

Meanwhile, Lackey was getting out of prison and Lisa was planning on getting married to her new boyfriend George; on their wedding night they ended up renting a hotel room in Kentucky.

My sisters Lavon, Tonya and I, went to the hotel that night to help them celebrate; I couldn't believe that somehow I was able to get in touch with Lackey and he also went with us to the hotel.

That night I had a wonderful time hanging out with him; it turned out to be fun and exciting; probably because we'd never went anywhere together; our relationship was strictly just sexual.

However, Lackey's sex drive wasn't what it used to be before he got locked up; somehow they must have given him too much salt peter; the stuff they supposedly gave men in prison to help keep their dicks from getting hard. However, I think maybe that stuff must have really messed him up because he just wasn't the same "Good Lover" that I was so accustom to being with!

Meantime, Lisa moved into another apartment and I met this guy that lived in her building who was a fire fighter; somehow we ended up dating and he turned out to be a really nice guy.

He had a real nice apartment and he always kept plenty of bomb ass weed on hand; he was quite the gentleman and knew how to treat a lady! However, he ended up moving out of my sister's building and eventually we lost contact with one another.

Meanwhile, I heard that David was home from the Navy and I really wanted to see him again. I asked his best friend Bob if he could bring him out to my apartment and he said that he would.

At that time Bob was married and his wife was pregnant; however, Bob said that "he didn't think that the baby was his because her months didn't add up to the time she got pregnant".

Meantime, Bob brought David to my apartment just like I asked him to; he also brought along Rick and some white girl. At first I thought that the girl was with either Rick or Bob because I just knew that she wasn't supposed to be with David. No way!

However, I found out that she was with David and I almost lost it. Oh no he didn't bring another bitch up in my face; I just couldn't believe that he played me like that. # Hell to the No!

I was so hurt and upset that I told Rick, David, and the white girl to get the hell up out of my apartment but told Bob to stay; that night I didn't want to be left alone! I needed a shoulder to cry on!

However that night I had ulterior motives of payback and revenge! I planned on sleeping with Bob to get back at David for bringing that girl to my house; also to try and make him jealous!

My plan was to give Bob these pills to drug him and take full advantage of him and somehow my plan worked. That night we had sex one time and the rest of the night I cried on his shoulders! However, sleeping with him was the biggest mistake I ever made!

Meanwhile, Lisa got a new car and gave me her old Nova; I finally had transportation of my own and didn't have to depend on anyone anymore; giving me that car was truly a huge blessing!

I started working at this nursing home in their dietary department and was hired to work a split shift. I had to be on my job at six o'clock every morning and work for a few hours then come back later to work for a few more hours. Split shift sucked!

After a while working the split shift really took its toll on me and I started getting sick for some reason; the smells of food made me sick to my stomach; I felt like throwing up all of the time!

However, I had the coolest boss ever and she didn't mind if sometimes I was late; but for some reason she just kept telling me "that she thought I was pregnant"; I told her that she was out of her damn mind and it was no way in hell that I was pregnant.

Meantime as more time passed I continued to get sicker and sicker! The more that I smelled the foods at my job was the sicker I became! It was then time to see if my boss prediction was right.

However, I went to the doctor and he did confirm that I was indeed pregnant! Bob somehow managed to knock my ass up only after doing it with him that onetime; this can't be happening!

I just couldn't wrap my head around the fact that he'd gotten me pregnant so fast. Why him; why Bob of all people...? All those years that I tried to get pregnant and couldn't ...What the hell...?

This definitely wasn't how it was supposed to turn out; I was only trying to make David jealous but I guess my plan backfired and I was devastated and totally shocked by what was going on!

This just goes to show...You can't always pick & choose who you want your child's father to be; especially if you lay down unprotected. You never know who or when God will pick out your baby's daddy...? It might not be the one that you want it to be!

However, I still had no idea if David or Lackey was my first child's father...? Then to get pregnant by David's best friend Bob; what a low down dirty shame and the shame was all on me!

Meanwhile, Bob and his wife were having some problems; he asked if he could stay with me for a little while. I didn't want to be in a relationship with him but I let him stay with me anyhow; I guess because I just didn't want to raise another child by myself!

Things between us started off ok but they soon turned sour once he finally realized that I was still madly in love with David and not in love with him; this was when everything started to change between us; however, this change wasn't for the better!

Somehow Bob started becoming really jealous and insecure; his jealousy caused him to start drinking really heavy and his behavior became a nightmare; he accused me of everything!

He accused me of having sex with my nephews; he also accused me of doing cocaine with my sister. However, it was all in his head; I wasn't doing any of the things he accused me of doing!

Meantime, he gave me a black eye for no reason! After my mother saw my eye she didn't want me having his baby anymore! Somehow she felt I should get rid of my baby and abort it at once!

She felt that Bob was too much like my father and she didn't want me to end up like her with a man that gets drunk and wants to put his hands on you; I didn't want a man like that either!

However, my mother had the nerves to try and take me to get an abortion! Not this time mother; this time I was well aware that I was pregnant. It was no way in hell I was going to let her make me kill my own flesh & blood again! She may have fooled me once but shame on her twice; this time I knew much better!

I wasn't fifteen and naïve anymore; she couldn't force me to kill another baby ever again! I may not have wanted Bob's baby but I sure as hell wasn't going to destroy another life ever again!

Meantime, Bob's jealousy got so out of control he became really paranoid. He'd come home from work empting out all the garbage cans and throw trash all over the floors looking for any clues to see if anyone was in the apartment while he was gone!

He also checked the kitchen sink to see how many glasses were used. Even though I had quit smoking he'd still checked the ashtrays for any weed cocktails or any kind of cigarette butts.

But the worst part of it all was when he smelled my panties to check for any signs of me having sex! However, this behavior went on for a long time until he drove me to my breaking point; I just couldn't take him accusing me of everything anymore!

However, by him kept on accusing me it somehow made me really want to go out and do something; so I had an affair with the guy who lived next door. However during this time somehow Bob caught a sexual transmitted disease and because of the affair that I was having I thought maybe I was the one who gave it to him!

I was so scared because I couldn't afford to have any kind of diseases while being pregnant. I immediately rushed to the doctor and he gave me a clean bill of health; it didn't come from me Bob!

Somehow I've always been the type that hated guys wearing rubbers; I liked feeling the warmth of the flesh inside of me; whoever I'd slept with had to be free from having any diseases!

From that point on it was no way in hell that I was going to sleep with Bob again without him wearing a rubber; unless I was absolutely sure that I was the only one he was messing with! It was common sense that I wasn't the only one messing around.

Bob had to either be messing with his wife or some other little, ratchet ass, easy bake oven hoe; because it damn sure wasn't me that burned him! # He better ask somebody!

Meanwhile, I moved out of my parent's neighborhood and moved to the city; I really didn't want to move but I received section eight housing and found an apartment that accepted it.

Bob asked if he could stay with me until he found a place; he didn't want to go back to his wife! However, for the sake of his unborn child I ended up letting him stay with me again!

What I found to be really strange was he never claimed his wife's baby until I started showing with my child and that's when he all of the sudden decided to claim him; I wondered why...?

His wife worked at a bank around the corner from my new place; he must have given her my new phone number because she started calling my house every day constantly harassing me!

She'd call my house every five minutes talking about her son needed this, her son needed that! After a while it became old news; she used her son as an excuse to gain control over Bob!

I just couldn't figure out why he just wouldn't go back to her; it came to the point that I gave him an ultimatum; it was going to be me or his wife because he damn sure wasn't having the both of us; that wasn't happening! Not on my watch it wasn't; # choose!

However, I wasn't tolerating his wife disrespecting me anymore; coming at me all sideways. I'd rather he just go back to her and leave me the hell alone; baby or not. # Bye, bye Bob!

Meantime, his wife drove me to my breaking point; I wanted to go to her job and confront her and give her a piece of my mind! Here I was pregnant and it was freezing cold outside with six inches of snow on the ground and I was headed to his wife's job!

However, he followed me and tried to stop me from going; he pushed me down in all that cold snow! There we were out there rolling around like two fools! I guess it didn't matter that I was carrying his child because he still wanted to wrestle with me!

Meanwhile one day Bob, Lavon and I went to visit a friend of Lavon's named Mr. Rump. When we arrived Bob and my sister wanted to go to Kentucky to get a bottle of liquor and come back.

However, I didn't want to go because I didn't feel so good. I asked Mr. Rump if I could stay there till they returned; he said I could wait for them in his guest room. He was a much older man and had no interest in me what so ever and the same went here!

I decided to take him up on his offer and went and laid down. Somehow when they got back Bob had already been drinking; he came to the guest room tripping and acting like a raving lunatic!

He started accusing me of having sex with Mr. Rump and kept insisting that I had fucked him! I was almost five months pregnant but he didn't seemed to care; he still acted like an idiot. Popping off for no reason; acting like a childish, jealous crazy fool.

Mr. Rump said something to him about his behavior and asked him to stop fighting with me and leave me alone! However Bob didn't stop; he just kept right on acting crazy! Mr. Rump said if "he didn't leave his house he was going to go get his gun out".

But Bob just kept right on trying to fight me so Mr. Rump pulled out his gun and Bob tried to grab it out of his hand. They got into a big scuffle and somehow the gun accidentally went off; Bob got shot and for some reason I thought he got shot in his eye!

However, even after he was shot and bleeding all over the place he was still chasing after me trying to fight me. I started running because I didn't want to see him with his eye shot out!

Lavon called the police and when the ambulance arrived that's when I realized that he didn't get shot in the eye; he was shot in the neck instead but I was too upset to go to the hospital.

Meantime, his family started calling me and trying to find out what happened and why he got shot. I tried explaining to them that he brought it upon himself and it wasn't Mr. Rumps fault.

However, his twin sister was the main one blaming me for her brother getting shot. I guess she thought that I told Mr. Rump to shoot him...? Meantime, Bob was doing ok but the doctors said that "he was lucky because the bullet just missed a vital organ"!

He wanted me to visit him in the hospital but I knew his family was going to be there; I sent Lavon up to his room to check things out. I didn't want to deal with any of his family because I knew that they all held me responsible for what happened to him!

Lavon came back and said that "all of his family members were waiting for me to show up; they were convinced that it was all my fault and once I showed up they planned on jumping me".

After hearing that I decided not to go see Bob that day. However, his family needed to know the real reason why he really got shot; the truth was because it was his own drunken fault.

Meantime, I was faced with another court trial; I was called by the prosecution to testify against Mr. Rump. It was no way that I was going to let that old man go down for something that wasn't his fault; after I gave my testimony he got off on self-defense!

Meanwhile, my sister Tonya moved in with me and I really enjoyed her company. Most of all I enjoyed her color television; I always wanted a color TV but was never able to afford one!

Meantime, when I was a little over six months pregnant I started spotting blood; the doctors were concerned it might be because of my after-birth was trying to come before the baby!

I was placed in a high risk clinic for the remaining of my pregnancy and the doctors ran all kinds of tests on me; but for some reason they couldn't seem to figure out what was going on!

Meanwhile, my due date was supposed to be March twenty-ninth but it was already into April. Somehow I guess the baby didn't want to come out of me! However, on April, 10th 1980 I gave birth to another baby girl & once again that Ouija board was right!

I named her Monica Renee and Bob signed her birth certificate to give her his last name. Her first name came from the character Monica from the soap opera General hospital and her middle name came from my favorite cousin Nee-Nee!

Two weeks after I gave birth I started bleeding really heavy! However, this bleeding wasn't normal and it wasn't my period. My father rushed me to the emergency room and by the time I got there I'd lost a lot of blood and I almost hemorrhaging to death!

The hospital gave me an emergency D&C to help stop the bleeding; I was hooked up to all these different types of machines and I felt really weak. Most of my family came to see me and they all said that from having lost so much blood I looked very pale!

That night the nurse told me to try and get some rest after my family left the hospital. However, I had this really bad feeling that if I went to sleep that I wasn't going to wake back up again!

I closed my eyes for just a second and laid there listening to my heartbeat on the monitor; however, as soon as I shut my eyes I heard the monitor go beep, beep, then there was a long beep! The nurse rushed over to me and I heard her yell out "code red".

Somehow my heart had stopped beating and I had flat lined. The doctor snatched the pillow from underneath my head and grabbed the paddles to try and start my heart back beating again!

Somehow at that very moment I must have had an outer body experience! I remember floating onto the ceiling and watching the doctor's as they worked on me! It was as if I were looking at myself in my own dream. However, it's hard to explain but I can say it was a remarkable and unbelievable experience!

I couldn't understand how it was so dark up on that ceiling but yet it was extremely bright looking down at myself; I can't explain how that was even possible; # it was truly magnificent.

Somehow I'd returned back to my body and I remember hearing the heart monitor start back beeping again. When I opened up my eyes I saw the doctor standing over me! He told me "he wasn't going to let me die" and that's when he ordered me eight or nine units of blood; I would have died without that blood!

Somehow after receiving my blood transfusion I was never the same anymore! It felt like I'd been given some old person's blood; I started feeling tired all of the time! I seriously believe that once a person receives another person's blood that somehow they'll never be the same anymore! # At least in my case I wasn't.

After my blood transfusion I was still having some bleeding; the doctors wanted me to remain in the hospital for a little while longer and my mother cared for my children while I was away!

However, after having my first baby she remained in the hospital and I developed a bad case of depression that caused me not to go bond with her! However, since I had to remain in the hospital myself I didn't bond with my second baby either! I just hate that I didn't get the chance to bond with either one of my babies! I was so disappointed and highly upset about this; # "☹"

The doctors said "if I continued bleeding that they may have to give me a partial hysterectomy or remove my entire womb and this would cause me not to be able to ever have any more kids".

Meantime, I finally stopped bleeding enough to get discharged from the hospital but instead of going straight home and getting into bed I ended up going to the grocery store instead!

While I was in the store I felt myself bleeding again so I immediately pushed my grocery cart aside and went straight home and laid it down; it was no way that I wanted the doctor's to take out my uterus; I had to be able to still have more children!

Meanwhile, I had a follow-up appointment with the doctors at the high risk clinic and Lavon came along with me; however both of us discovered some very shocking news that day!

The doctors informed us that "I had a miscarriage and the fetus was fully developed with no bones"…Say what…? I didn't understand what the hell the doctors were talking about; I recently just had a baby and she was perfectly fine with all of her bones!

However, apparently when I was around six months pregnant somehow I got pregnant again and the other fetus got pushed behind my ribcage somehow; therefore the sonogram was never able to detect the other baby that was inside of me!!!

Damn what kind of super sperm did Bob have…? I know he was a twin but somehow he got me pregnant twice!! Wow!!!

This explains why I started bleeding when I was pregnant and the doctors couldn't figure out why; it was because the other fetus was inside of me and somehow it came out from behind my ribcage and aborted itself two weeks after I gave birth to Monica!

The high risk clinic had all of this information concerning my miscarriage and the size of the fetus listed in my medical records; everything concerning my medical situation was inside that chart!

Something that day told me to just walk out the clinic and take my medical chart with me but instead I ended up turning it back in; I should have followed my first mind and kept my chart.

Meanwhile, I turned twenty-four years old…However, after giving birth to my second daughter somehow I never got my period again! Somehow my hormones were still all messed up!

My grandmother, my father's mother passed away; may God bless her soul. However during that time I didn't get to go to her funeral because my oldest daughter had the chicken pox's!

Meantime, I became really close with Bob's cousin Freeda and her daughter Lannie; she was crazy about her little cousin and she became her anytime babysitter. Thanks Lannie!

However, Bob was still acting like a crazy jealous fool. His drinking got so out of control it caused him to do stupid stuff. Not only did he do stupid stuff to me he did it to other people as well.

One day, Tonya and Lavon's friend Pat came over and everyone was drinking and playing cards; somehow Bob knocked Pat down a flight of stairs in the building where I lived!

However, she was ok and decided not to press any charges on him! Lucky you Bob; if that would have been me you'd still be locked up in jail somewhere because that was totally uncalled for!

Meanwhile, Tonya moved out and Bob's cousin Freeda started staying with me. Somehow, Lackey found out where I lived and he started coming over to wreck more havoc on my life!

However, Lackey was the last person that I wanted coming around because of how jealous Bob was; since I knew Lackey would cause trouble I told Freeda about how he destroyed my other past relationships and she understood and offered to help!

One day Lackey knocked on my door and Freeda said "let her handle it"! She opened my door and somehow she was able to get rid of him! She never told Bob and kept that information to herself; she knew how her cousin would react. Thanks Freeda!

Meanwhile, I decided to move out of the city and move back near my parents in an apartment that was only fifteen minutes away from their house; I also found a job ten minutes away.

I was hired by the Red Roof Inn as a housekeeper. I got along with all my co-workers and it was a really fun place to work. I made friends with a few ladies named Evelyn, Hattie and a young lady named Sharon; we all became really close friends.

All of the housekeepers wore these tee-shirts that said "sleep cheap" written on them. However, we started getting a lot of negative comments from some of the male guest about that sleep cheap motto! Some of the men teased us about that saying.

However, those negative comments became so bad that the Red Roof Inn ended up changing their "sleep cheap" motto to something else that was much more appropriate!

Meanwhile, I turned twenty-five years old…One day I received a very disturbing phone call from my father saying that my mother had somehow passed out on their kitchen floor and he was waiting for an ambulance to arrive!

Bob and I quickly rushed to my parent's house and when we arrived the paramedics were already working on her. However my mother wasn't responding to any of the treatment and it didn't look good! I had this real gut feeling she wasn't going to make it. # "☹"

She was taken to the hospital and announced dead upon arrival. However, I believe that she died on her kitchen floor that day! She suffered a heart attack and I soon realized that I had lost my mother forever! Just like that she was gone from this world!!!

I remember kissing her on her cheek the day of her funeral; however, the kiss of death is something that I will never forget. It was the strangest feeling that I'd ever felt in my life; it was so cold.

Before they closed my mother's casket I whispered into her ear to "tell my un-born baby that I was sorry and didn't know any better when I was forced to take all those pills; I'm so sorry baby"!

I was standing outside the church after the funeral was over and somehow a bee flew up my dress and stung me on my ass! However, somehow I think the bee was really my mother's spirit trying to tell me something! God bless her soul and forgive her for making me kill Tony's unborn child; # I will forever regret doing it!

Meanwhile, life went on and my father brought my sister Vet this mini-scooter. We road all over town and attracted lots of attention from guys that were always trying to get their holla on!

We met my next door neighbor Markie; he was a married man and had a daughter the same age as my oldest daughter and they became best friends and often spend the night together.

During this time things were really, really bad between me and Bob. I was very unhappy being with him but I continued dealing with his bull-shit only for the sake of our daughter.

One day Markie came over to pick up his daughter and my cat had just had kittens; he was thinking about getting one for his daughter. I was holding one of the kittens on my lap when he started rubbing and playing with it. However, the next thing I knew was somehow he started rubbing on my thigh instead.

I was totally shocked and it caught me way off guard; I wasn't expecting for him to do that especially since Bob was sitting right there next to me and I prayed that Bob didn't see him!

Somehow after that little incident happened Markie and I started having an affair behind Bob and his wife's back; we would sneak over each other's apartment while they were gone to work!

We would have sex in both apartments; on the kitchen tables, the sinks, the counter tops, on the stoves, in the shower and almost anywhere we could think of; # we did it everywhere!

One day as I was staring out my window looking at Markie somehow Bob was right behind me but I didn't know that he was there. Bob saw how I looked at him and he took off his shoe and threw it at my head; somehow the shoe missed me and instead it ended up breaking out the glass on our daughter's picture!

My affair with Markie lasted a while but he ended up moving to another neighborhood. However, because of our daughter's friendship we still managed to keep in contact but eventually we lost touch with one another and I didn't see him anymore!

Meantime, my job was having a Christmas party and I decided to take Bob to the party; what I do that for...? I was hoping that he'd be on his best behavior but I should have known better. You can't teach an old dog new tricks; # they'll never learn!

At the party they had plenty of good food, music and drinks. I was having a good time until Bob got drunk. I decided to enter a dance contest and somehow I won 1st prize! Due to all the attention that I was getting somehow Bob got really jealous of me!

However, you would have thought that he'd be happy for me winning the contest but instead he tried to chock me! I ran into the ladies restroom and locked the door behind me! The head housekeeper and one of my supervisors were already in there.

Bob started banging on the bathroom door and screaming for me to come out. The head housekeeper went to get the head supervisor so that he could speak to him about his behavior and somehow he was able to calm Bob down after speaking to him!

Meanwhile, a year had gone by since I gave birth to my second child; I still never had my period after having that D&C. I scheduled a doctor's appointment to find out the reason why; they admitted me into the out-patient surgery to have some test ran!

They stuck this lighted scope inside of me to see what was going on. After running all the tests they said "I would never have to worry about having anymore periods ever again; also my tubes were sealed closed on both sides and it was no way to open them back up". This meaning I'll never be able to have any more kids!!!

No more periods I could see but no more kids I damn near lost it. I couldn't believe my ears; it was the most devastating and painful news that I ever wanted to hear! This can't be happening!!!

I was heartbroken and highly upset and I started getting very depressed all over again! I at least wanted to be able to have one more baby that I could possibly bond with and be happy with that child's father because unfortunately Bob just wasn't that one!

Although I already had two children I still wanted more! Not to mention the fact that I still didn't know whether or not if David or Lackey was Heather's father; then to be in love with David and get pregnant by his best friend Bob; # this was an abomination!

This was the point in my life when salt got dumped into all of my open wounds; the biggest wound of them all was when my mother forced me to kill Tony's unborn child. I felt that God was definitely punishing me for all of my past actions and mistakes!!!

---∞✦∞---

Meanwhile, when I turned twenty-six years old...My oldest daughter was almost seven years old; her teacher wanted me to have her tested because she noticed things that concerned her!

She said "sometimes she would see my daughter staring into space and thought that she may be having Twilight seizures". However, I've never witnessed any of the things that her teacher was saying and I had no idea what she was even talking about.

Meanwhile, Pamela Jean's mother passed away and I dreaded going to her funeral; may God bless her. Soon after Pamela Jean lost her mother she went away to New Orleans.

However, she brought back a souvenir of a lifetime; she came back pregnant with a baby boy and named him Jamie. A year later Lavon gave birth to a baby girl and named her Tamara.

I was so happy for them but at the same time I was sad for myself. I was still trying to wrap my head around what the doctors told me about not being able to have any more children! However, this caused me to be stricken with lots of grief and mass regrets!!!

Meanwhile, Sade helped me get a job as a private duty nurse's assistance; I kept my job at the motel and worked both jobs. The job was really easy; all I had to do was listen out for an elderly man to ring his little bell whenever he needed something.

However, one day it was extremely hot outside and earlier that day me and my co-workers at the motel had been drinking and smoking weed; somehow I got messed up; I got really high!

I was coming down off my high when I arrived at my second job and it was nice and cool inside from the air conditioner; this caused me to become really relaxed and I passed out and didn't hear the man ringing his little bell and I ended up getting fired.

Meantime, things on my job at the motel were off the chain; all sorts of craziness was going on! One guest paid Evelyn four hundred dollars just to get him a spoon to cook his cocaine on.

Another guest came to the motel to give herself a coat hanger abortion! After that happened none of us housekeepers wanted to clean up that room; # it was a bloody, disgusting, mess!

Also a well-known local judge committed suicide in one of the rooms; people started calling the motel "the Dead Roof Inn."

Meanwhile, my hormones were still all screwed up and there were no signs of my periods ever returning! Somehow I guess the doctors were right about me never having another period again!

Bob continued to be abusive toward me and I was still very unhappy being in a relationship with him so I ended up having an affair with the maintenance guy from my job named Davey!

I had the biggest crush on him way before we even hooked up! He was this really cute white guy who was exciting and fun to be around! He was a breath of fresh air and he was the first white guy that I'd ever been with but I was definitely down with the swirl.

However, I owed it all to the head housekeeper because she was the reason how we ended up hooking up together! Whenever I needed extra help cleaning my rooms she'd stick me with Davey instead of letting one of the other female housekeepers help me!

Davey and I started having sex on and off the job; we must have did it in every room at that motel. My sister didn't live far from my job and sometimes we hung out over there. However, I had to be extra careful so Bob wouldn't find out about my affair!

Meanwhile, there was a young white housekeeper named Karen and she also had a crush on Davey! Sometimes we hung out together but she had no idea that I was having sex with him.

One day Karen didn't show up for work and she didn't call in. Later that day the job got a phone call saying that "she was dead"! She was found shot inside her car but the police had evidence that someone had placed her body in the car after she was shot. The police questioned everyone on the job concerning her death!

The head housekeeper had the nerves to ask me "if I'd killed Karen". Are you serious …? I couldn't believe that she would ask me something that crazy and outrageous; # what I look like…?

Just because Karen and I both liked the same guy it didn't mean that I would kill her! No I'm not a cold-blooded killer or some maniac; I could see if she was just kidding but she was dead serious when she asked me that! Who did she think I was…?

Meanwhile, I became the neighborhood nanny and the cat lady; I found myself always surrounded by lots of children and lots of cats; somehow it helped me forget about my medical problem!

Meantime, I spoke to a lawyer about my medical situation and he thought it sounded like I had a potential lawsuit. However, when I went to the hospital to get a copy of all my medical records somehow all the records weren't in my medical file!

However, nowhere in my records were the papers that I saw concerning a fetus with no bones; somehow those records were missing! When I asked the lady in the record department for the rest of my records she said "she'd already given me everything that was supposed to be in my files." # No... Not everything!!!

Oh hell no; where were the rest of my files that I saw when I went to the high risk clinic that day...? I guess somehow I must have waited too long before going to get a copy of those records! It had been a year later and somehow those records mysteriously disappeared. What the hell is going on up in that hospital...?

However, the kicker part was the reason that they'd listed for the cause of my bleeding that almost caused me to bleed to death; somehow it was listed as being post-partum hemorrhaging!

Nothing what-so-ever was listed in those medical records about another fetus being left inside of me; or that I'd supposedly had a miscarriage two weeks after I gave birth to my second child.

Everyone I knew said "they believed that the hospital purposely removed those files from my records because they also knew that it could have been a possible lawsuit against them!"

I hated that I didn't follow my first mind when I went to the clinic that day and saw all that incriminating evidence; I should have taken my chart when I had the chance to! Well it's too late now because everything I saw in that file had been removed!

Meanwhile, I turned twenty-seven years old... I guess the doctors were right about me never having another period.

However, each month I started having these really bad cramps and it felt like my period was trying to come back down. I didn't know what was going on and I tried to ignore the pain!

I thought maybe it was gas trapped inside of my womb so I tried taking several over the counter medications but nothing seemed to work so every month I continued to deal with the pain!

Meantime, Bob's drinking became more out of control and his jealousy worsen; I was finally at my breaking point and I was fed up with his abusive behavior; I just couldn't take it no more!

I tried talking to him and letting him know that I wanted out of our relationship. I wanted him to move out but somehow he didn't want to leave; instead he started becoming more violent with me!

Bob's suspicion about me messing around with the white guy became really obvious and he tried to beat me up every chance he got. I became scared of him and frightened that if I didn't get away from him that somehow he'd seriously hurt me!

This was the point when I borrowed my sister's gun; I wasn't going to shoot him I just wanted to give him a little scare! He'd already got shot once in his lifetime and you would have thought it was enough; however, maybe somehow it wasn't...?

One day Bob kept taunting with me for no reason; I asked him to leave me alone but he refused. I pulled out the gun and fired it towards the wall. He had no idea that I even had a gun; I was able to surprise him with a rude awakening. # Wake up Bob!

However, even after I shot at him he still didn't want to leave! That next day I packed all of his shit and like Beyonce said in her song; "to the left, to the left, everything you own is in a box to the left"! Bob must not knew about me; he better go ask somebody!

I changed my locks and called a cab and told the driver to drop off all of his things in the front lobby on his job; then I called the junk yard down the street and sold them his broken down car!

Meantime, Bob came back with the part for his car but it was gone and he was furious with me! I knew he wanted to kill me but I did what I had to do; besides his child needed some things! After that he took back everything that he'd ever given to me; oh well.

Meanwhile, his check came inside my mailbox and I called to see if he was willing to help me out financially but he was still on some dumb shit so I decided not to tell him about his check.

Instead I took matters into my own hands and deposited it into the bank; after the check cleared I withdrew all the money out of the account! I felt that our daughter was rightfully entitled to every dime of that money whether Bob thought so or not.

I continued messing around with Davey until he decided to move to Texas with his family; after he left I went back into a deep depression and became isolated again. I stayed in the house and didn't want to go anywhere or do anything! Just leave me alone!

Meanwhile, my friend Deb and her two daughters, Tanika and Tammy needed a place to stay; I told them that since I was finally rid of Bob they were more than welcome to stay with me!

JP lived around the corner and Deb was always going over there; she'd always come back telling me about some cute guy that lived in JP's building and wanted me to see him for myself.

However, after what I'd just gone through with Bob I wasn't interested in seeing anyone else! I truly missed my white boo but he moved out of town and I just didn't want to see any other man.

I was at the point in my life where I didn't want to be bothered with anymore men; I was done with them and had sworn them off completely! At least at the time that's what I thought.

Meanwhile, four years had passed by and I still hadn't had a period since giving birth to my last child. I refused to believe that the doctors were right about me never having anymore periods or having any more children! I just couldn't accept that; no way!

Somehow, I was still having those pains each month and they started getting so severe that it became really unbearable to deal with. It was time to finally go to the doctor to find out what was causing them because I just couldn't ignore them anymore!

However, when I used the restroom I saw something very disturbing a few weeks before my doctor's appointment. I saw all this black stuff coming out of me! What the hell is going on now..?

CHAPTER 3

Biological Ticking Time Bomb

A hopeless journey >> to Self-Destruction!!!

* Mid-life Crisis*

* Fifty One & Time 2 Let It Go*

* Memories and events: from ages: 28-51*

Meanwhile, I turned twenty-eight years old… This was another turning point in my life and somehow destiny took control again and all I could do was sit back and roll with the flow!

It's been over four years since I saw my last period and I was told that "I'll never have another period in my lifetime"! I was waiting to see a doctor to find out why this black stuff was still coming out of me; I needed to know exactly what this stuff was!

Somehow a few days before my doctor's appointment the black stuff turned red; somehow it was my period coming back! However, the black stuff was all that old blood coming out of me!

In spite of what those doctors told me four years ago they were wrong because somehow I was back bleeding again! The doctor's wanted to find out what was going on with me so they schedule an appointment to have some more test ran.

However, all of the doctors were very baffled about my period returning! One of them even said "my medical situation was very unusual and out of his fifty years of practice that he had never seen a case like mines before"!

Meantime, while waiting to have my outpatient surgery Deb continued telling me about this cute guy that lived in JP's building. I was so sick and tired of hearing about him I decided to go see him for myself; I wanted to know what all the fuss was about!

One day after getting off work my co-worker Hattie and I stopped by JP's to see what was so amazing about this guy that Deb kept raving about. What was so special about him...?

When we first arrived at JP's, Deb was already looking out the window staring at him; finally I was about to see for myself. We all were peeking out the window trying to get a good look at him. I was curious to know why Deb couldn't shut up about him.

However, after seeing him I saw why she couldn't shut up! He was this very handsome, light skinned guy with a head full of long beautiful hair. I could tell that he worked out because he had muscles and looked very buff. When he saw us watching him in the window he had the nerves to start flexing his chest muscles!

Although I wasn't into light-skinned guys somehow I found him very attracted. I guess after being with a white guy it must have somehow changed my mind towards the light skinned guys.

However, I wasn't interested in getting involved with anyone else; I didn't dare want to start another relationship with no other man! Being in another relationship was the last thing on my mind.

At that point the only thing that a man could do for me was to get me pregnant; especially since my period started back again! I felt that it was still hope on becoming pregnant once again!

Meanwhile, Connie's brother Bo passed away; my sister Lisa asked me to go with her to his funeral. I hadn't planned on going simply because of what happened between Bo and I that time!

I told Lisa I'd go ahead and go for her sake; the reason why she wanted to go was to support her best friend Sheila because she had a son by Bo named Goodness. However, it never dawned on me that Bo's cousin Walden would also be there.

When we first arrived at the funeral the first person I saw was Connie's brother's Ike; sitting next to him was none other than Walden himself; however, he had no idea who I even was!

He asked his cousin who I was and Ike responded "nigga you know who that is; that's O'Gram". Walden was so shocked because we hadn't seen each other since Connie's funeral.

We hadn't interacted with one another since he dumped me when he thought that I'd betrayed him with Lackey at age fifteen! However, he had gotten married and had four beautiful daughters.

After the funeral he asked if we could go to my place so that we could talk; he wanted to catch up on what been going on in each other's lives. I was a little skeptical about taking him to my place because he was married and deeply involved in the church!

I was too afraid that I still might have had some un-resolved feelings for him after we broke up because I never got the chance to resolve those feelings after our relationship got destroyed.

I suggested that we go get something to eat and go visit Pamela Jean instead of going to my place. I didn't trust myself and I didn't want to take any chances being alone with him!

I will admit that in my past I was like a magnet for married men and yes I had my share of them! However, I wasn't trying to become a home wrecker; at least not at that time I wasn't.

Walden and I got the chance to talk about everything and after we departed our ways there were no expectations between us! However, he did ask for my number to keep in touch with me.

Meanwhile, Deb and I made this bet with one another; the bet was to see who could sleep with the cute guy first. Little did I know; that somehow I'd be the one that sleeps with him first.

It happened one Father's Day night after me, Deb, JP and our kids were coming home from the amusement park; after I dropped JP off we saw the cute guy walking his dog outside.

I said to myself let the games begin and the bet was on. I was more than willing and ready and determined to win the bet that Deb and I had made! It was time to get it on and poppin!

First I had to come up with a plan on how I was going to accomplish getting this guy into bed with me; of course my first plan was to try and get him high and seduce him into having sex!

However, earlier we'd smoked all of our weed up so I asked Deb and JP for money so that I could go get a dime bag. Then I boldly approached this guy and started a conversation with him.

He said his name was CC and his dog's name was Rocky. I asked him if he smoked weed and if he wanted to get high with us and somehow he answered yes to both of my questions.

I asked him if he'd still be outside when I came back and he said yes so I left and took a ride and went to go get the weed; when I returned he was right there waiting for me! We all smoked a few joints and then it was time to get rid of Deb and JP!

CC took his dog inside and said he'd be right back. I was so determined to win the bet with Deb that I asked JP if I could borrow her keys to her apartment so that I could take him inside!

She gave me her keys but said "it was no way that she was waiting outside"; I suggested they all wait for me at my place. I had my sister's car that night because mines was broken. Neither Deb nor JP had a driver's licenses but I told them to take the car anyway and wait for me at my apartment until I called them.

Deb really didn't want to leave because she knew that I was about to win our bet; she was also scared to drive my sister's car without having a driver's license. However, I begged her to leave and somehow I was able to convince her to do so.

When CC came back outside I took the rest of the weed and I immediately grabbed him by his hand and led him straight to JP's apartment. It was about to go down & it was no turning back!

As soon as we got inside of JP's apartment something told me to ask him if he was married, single or divorce or had any girlfriends...? He said "he was married"; oh boy here I go again!

"Married" I said; I didn't see that coming! Then he said "his wife was downstairs asleep in their apartment". I asked if he was legally married or if he was just in a common law marriage...?

Unfortunately he said he was legally married; boy was I shocked. In my head I was thinking lord help me not another married man! However, since I knew it was only going to be just a one night stand I said what the hell I'll go for it anyway!

I was so attracted to him and I was really hoping to prove the doctors wrong by trying to get pregnant by him. I thought I'd kill two birds with one stone; win the bet and also get pregnant.

It seemed like ever since my mother forced me to self-abort my unborn child that I've been on some kind of mission to become pregnant 24\7. However, after the doctors told me that I couldn't have no more kids I became even more screwed up!

I prayed that the doctors were wrong about me not being able to have any more kids; especially since they were wrong about me never having anymore periods ever again. But yet four years later somehow my period mysteriously returned again.

Anyhow, my plan was to go ahead and sleep with CC but never ever see him again; even if that meant never going back over JP's apartment again! Whatever it took not to see him again!

After we finished having some really great sex I called Deb to come back and get me. I left JP's apartment that night with all the intentions in the world on never seeing CC ever again!

The only thing that he knew about me was my first name; I didn't give him my phone number or tell him anything about me! As far as I was concerned that was it. I'd won the bet with Deb and hopefully somehow he had put a baby inside of me!

After I got home Deb and I discussed our bet that we made; whoever lost the bet had to babysit for a month. Since I was the one that slept with CC first that meant she owed me a month's worth of watching my kids! Ha-ha Deb time to pay up!

Meantime, sometimes later on Deb said that "she could have slept with CC the day before I slept with him; if only she had five more minutes alone with him and she would have won our bet"!

However, CC said "it was no way in hell that he would have ever slept with her; five more minutes or not"! However, I Guess I'll never know which one of them was telling the truth…?

Meanwhile, Walden called and started coming over taking me different places; he did whatever he could to help me and my girls out; he also baked these delicious homemade rolls for us.

Bob also started coming back around trying to be a father to his daughter. One day he saw Walden at my house and he got a serious attitude; however, it wasn't a damn thing that he could do or say about anything anymore; those days were long over!

However, as time passed my feelings for Walden got even stronger; somehow I let my heart take control over my actions and I wanted him back in my life again! Somehow I didn't care about his wife and children anymore; I was determined to win him back!

One day Walden came to visit me and I remember getting butt naked and calling him into my bedroom. However, by him being deeply involved in the church I just knew he'd probably wouldn't have sex with me or commit adultery on his wife!

When he first came into my bedroom and saw that I was butt naked he was shocked. He said "as bad as he wanted to have sex with me he just couldn't"; after he turned me down I was hurt!

I started crying my eyes out and couldn't stop; I tried telling him that no one would ever have to know but us. He said "God would know and he couldn't betray his wife and kids that way"!

Although I didn't want to hear what he was saying I had to respect his decision anyhow but I wasn't giving up without a fight.

However, after trying to seduce him, he really felt that I needed some strength and spiritual guidance in my life! He asked me if my girls and I would like to attend his Church one Sunday.

I said sure I'd love to attend your church but in the back of my mind I was still scheming on what I could do to win him back into my life again! I had a personal agenda going on in my head.

Meantime, Deb went behind my back and told him about my plans to wreck his marriage; she warned him to be extra cautious of me! However, at the time I had no idea she even told him that.

Meanwhile, Deb finally got her license and one day I let her use my car to go over JP's. I was in a desperate state of mind and I couldn't help but to think about my situation with Walden.

That day I just wanted to be left alone and didn't feel like being bothered with anyone! I was walking around the house looking like a total bum and my hair was sticking all over my head.

Later that evening when I looked outside my window I saw Deb coming back from JP's. When I looked again I saw CC laying on the top of the hood of my car. I thought to myself what is he doing here…? I'm going to kill Deb for bringing him to my house!

I ran really fast to put on my clothes and I tried to comb my hair before she came inside; she immediately start trying to explain why CC was with her. She knew that I didn't want him ever finding out where I lived or anything about me for that matter!

After CC informed me that he was legally married I never wanted to see him ever again! At least that's what I thought but Deb said that "he insisted that she showed him where I lived at".

Somehow he got on top of the car and refused to get off; Deb had to end up driving all the way from JP's apartment with him on top of the hood. Lord please help me I'm going to need it!

However, as Deb and I were talking somehow CC climbed onto my balcony and let himself inside my apartment; somehow he was back in my life whether I wanted him to be or not. OMG!

Meanwhile, I received a call from Walden saying that he wanted my girls and me to come to church that Sunday; somehow his wife was on the other end listening to our phone conversation.

Walden told me "after his wife overheard us talking she went out and bought a new outfit and got her hair and nails done". I guess she wanted to look good for when I showed up at Church!

When we first arrived my girls and I sat in the very back of the Church and I saw Walden, his wife and their four daughters all sitting up in the front row looking like one big happy family!

However, in my heart I knew right then that I could no longer continue scheming to get him back into my life again! I knew I was no match for what God had joined together! I had to let him go and try to move on with my life just like I did when we were fifteen.

Meantime, he continued to visit me and somehow I was able to introduce him to CC. When I first introduced them I told CC that "Walden would always be a part of my life no matter what"!

I also said that "if he had any problems with that then I didn't think it would work out between us"! CC said "he had no problems with it and he understood how I felt about the matter."

However, after making that comment I thought that Walden would always be a part of my life but somehow he just upped and disappeared and I never saw or heard from him ever again!

Meanwhile, I discovered that the only thing that CC and I really had in common was the amazing sex; however, somehow I still ended up falling in love with him! Somehow he decided to leave his wife and somehow he ended up moving in with me!

CC was twenty-four years old; I was four years older than him. He was born under the Zodiac sign Aries on the border line of being a Taurus; maybe that's why we had nothing in common.

His wife was eighteen years old; she had a son the same age as my youngest daughter and they were in the same pre-school together; however, her son wasn't CC's biological child.

One day CC's wife somehow showed up at my door and she was crying; she said "she was pregnant and wanted to speak to her husband". In the back of my mind I was thinking damn that should have been me the one who was pregnant by him; not her!

I told her to go in my bed room so that they could talk in private; later when I went back to check on them his wife laid her head down on my lap and started crying again; she said "she needed CC to come back home so they could be a family again"!

However, I was still trying to figure out how his wife even knew where I lived at...? Later I found out that it was my own two daughters and Deb's two daughter's that told her where I lived.

One day the kids were over JP's and his wife saw them playing outside and somehow she was able to bribe them into telling her my address. # Sneaky heifer! I just couldn't believe that those kids sold me out for a few candy bars & a couple of dollars!

Meantime, CC decided to go back to be with his pregnant wife and I was devastated; I went back into a deep depression and I shut down! All I did was go to work, come home and sleep a lot. I barely ate and I didn't want to be bothered with anyone!

However, during that time Deb was a big help in looking after my kids; I wasn't in no condition to do so myself. She tried hard to get me out of my depression but nothing seemed to work!

I shut down for at least three months and then I decided to write CC a letter expressing how I really felt about him. I took the letter to his parent's house and gave it to his step-father.

His step-father said that "he would make sure that CC got my letter." I was hoping that after he got it that he'd come and see me; little did I know back then somehow he never got my letter!

Meantime, somehow CC still had my father's triple AAA card and he needed it back; however, getting the card back was the perfect excuse to go over his house and knock on his door.

One day Deb, the kids and I, went over JP's; I was hoping to see CC to get my father's card back; he lived in a basement apartment and I notice that one of his windows was cracked open.

At the time neither he nor his wife was at home. When I looked inside their bedroom window I thought I'd saw my father's card laying on the top of their dresser so I came up with this plan.

I looked at Deb and she looked at me and said "she hoped that I wasn't thinking about what she thought I was thinking"; but somehow I was thinking about it; about climbing in his window and getting my father's card back. I figured I'd just go in and grab it and save myself the trouble of having to see CC again!

Somehow I wasn't thinking about I'd be breaking & entering into someone else's apartment; however, I came up with another plan so that I wouldn't have to climb inside the window myself.

Instead I ended up getting the kids to climb inside for me; they unlocked his front door and I told Deb to be my lookout person while I went inside to get my father's card back.

After I got inside the card that I thought was my father's card wasn't his after all; so I looked around his apartment to see if maybe I could find it but I didn't see it nowhere in sight.

Somehow I did see a bag of weed so I decided to take that instead. I figured CC owed me that much for coming back into my life just so he could leave me again because that shit really hurt!

However that next day I went back over JP's and saw CC's car parked in their parking lot; I knew that I'd stolen his weed so I didn't want to knock on their door so I put a note on it instead. A few days passed and I was hoping that he would have brought the card back himself; somehow his wife brought it back instead.

Meantime, I was looking for another apartment; I wanted to move as far away from CC as I could. I should have never put myself out there like that; I knew much better not to get involved.

He was only supposed to be just a one night stand; I should have never let myself develop any real feelings for him. What the hell was I thinking...? I guess I just really wanted to get pregnant!

However, I couldn't blame nobody but myself for being in that messed up situation; my life was in a shambles and once again my heart was broken but I had to move on with my life!

Meanwhile on my job at the Red Roof Inn, little did I know that I was about to get the biggest shock of my life!!! Destiny had set up a cross road for me to see someone very special from my past; however, I wasn't sure if I'd be able to face this person!

It was one day I came into work and my boss said to make sure that all my rooms get cleaned really good that day because somehow they were expecting some celebrity guest to arrive!

However, that day somehow all of my rooms were really dirty and badly messed up but they planned on putting the celebrities on my station; I thought to myself why my station of all stations...?

That day I was also a total mess; I looked like somebody had dragged me through the ringer. I was on my period bleeding really heavy and I wasn't in no condition to see anybody that day!

Somehow it seemed like whenever I came on my period that nothing ever seemed to ever go right with me; especially when it came to dealing with my hair and skin; I was a hot mess dot com!

I was curious to know who the celebrities were that were coming in; we recently had La' Wanda Page, AKA Aunt Ester from the TV show "Sandford & Son" stayed there as a guest.

When I asked my boss who was coming he said "it was the singer Pebbles and the group the Deele's; they were putting on a concert in town and they were due to arrive at any moment".

Oh my Goodness I almost lost it when I heard that the Deele's were coming; I became so distraught that I could barely breathe! I felt this raging regret emerging deep down inside of me!

All sorts of things were running through my brain and I was so hysterical. I couldn't function or think straight less known clean any rooms that day; I got so weak hearing that Tony was coming!

I told my boss I needed help with cleaning my rooms; I just couldn't get myself together. I hadn't seen Tony since before my mother forced me to get rid of his baby. I didn't know what I was going to do or how was I going to face him after killing his baby!

Later on I saw a big tour bus pulling into the parking lot and I knew it had to be them; I didn't know how I was going to talk to him or how I was going to be able to look him straight in his eyes!

My first instinct was to run for cover and hide under a rock somewhere; no way did I want him to see me right then. However, this was the perfect opportunity to have that long overdue conversation that I was so destined to have with him.

I desperately needed some type of closure; also to find out what really happened between us after he got me pregnant in that Church. I still had no recollection of how we departed our ways...?

However, when they first arrived none of my rooms were cleaned and my boss ended up putting them on someone else's station. At that point I didn't know what to do; I thought that I could avoid him by trying to hide from him but somehow he spotted me!

I couldn't believe that after all those years he still recognize me; he knew exactly who I was! When he first approached me I thought I was going to piss my pants! I couldn't believe that the man whose baby I was forced to destroy was somehow at my job!

He came over to where I was working and said "after he settled in his room he'd be back out to talk to me." By then I was a complete nervous wreck; I was so shocked and embarrassed all at the same time but I was also very excited to see him again!

However, all sorts of thoughts were running through my head; I thought should I tell him about killing his baby or should I keep it to myself and take that secret to my grave...?

Later after he settled in his room he came back outside to talk to me! I remember sitting inside a car talking to him but for some reason I can't remember whose car it was...? All I can remember is that we did sit in a car and had a conversation.

However, this is where my story gets fuzzy again because I can't remember for the life of me what we talked about. For some strange reason I have blocked that conversation completely out of my mind; once again only Tony can tell you what we talked about.

I don't know if we talked about old times or how we hooked up behind JP's back; I don't know if I'd mention anything about killing his baby or not...? Only Tony himself has these answers!

Perhaps they're too painful for me to remember; somehow they're still locked deep down within my soul and only Tony has the key to unlocking all these un-answered questions within me!

However, the only thing that I do remember is EXACTLY how I felt that day. For one I remember feeling very guilty and full of shame and lots of regrets for being force to kill his unborn child!

That day I felt really self-conscious about my appearance; I also felt uneasy sitting in that car talking to him! I guess by me cleaning rooms for a living it somehow made me feel even more ashamed and embarrassed to be around him again!

I also felt beneath him and not worthy of having a conversation with him; I also felt that maybe I never meant nothing to him! I felt uncomfortable knowing that his wife was just a few feet away waiting patiently for him to return to their room!

However, even with all those negative feelings that I felt it was still great seeing him again! I just wished that our timing could have been better. Unfortunately his visit caught me way off guard and I wasn't at all prepared for his unexpected arrival that day.

That following day I didn't get the chance to see him before they checked out; he was already gone by the time I got to work. Somehow I was left without having any closure and I remember feeling very sad and full of deep regrets within my heart and soul.

Seeing Tony again affected me in a way that made me realize just how important it was for me to get pregnant again! All the regrets that I carried inside of me for all those years made me really want to replace the baby that I'd destroyed at age fifteen!

Meanwhile, I was still focusing on finding another apartment; I still wanted to move just in case CC tried to contact me again. However, one day out of nowhere he stopped by for a visit and somehow he ended up moving back in with me again!

He said "the baby that his wife was carrying wasn't his baby and he still wanted to be with me". However, I figured I'd still move so that his wife wouldn't be able to find us again.

Meantime, CC left out every morning going to work but never brought home any paychecks! I started wondering what was going on. The kids told me "during the time that he should have been at work they'd sometimes see him at his wife's place".

Also Deb told me "she ran into CC's wife and she told her that she and CC were still sleeping together." She called herself showing Deb some so-called evidence of the washcloth that he'd supposedly used after they had sex; # who does that...?

However, I wasn't born yesterday; I already knew that something wasn't right with him. Later I found out that he got fired from his job but had me thinking that he was still going to work; but in reality he was spending time with his wife! Didn't he know that I would eventually somehow find this out...?

As time passed by I told CC that I wasn't going to allow him to continue bouncing back and forth between me and his wife. I wasn't going to be his little side chick; I rather he just leave me alone! I wasn't going to be caught up in some kind of love triangle!

Meanwhile, CC eventually cut off all ties with his wife but she started harassing us; she started coming over to my apartment trying to do anything to get her husband back into her life again.

Somehow Bob also found out that CC was staying with me and he too started coming over harassing us! Between the two of them I don't know which one of them was the worse...?

It seemed like they were running a race to see which one could aggravate us the most. It got so bad that we couldn't even get a peace of mind so we decided to run away from home!

We went over Cindy's house just so we could escape the madness. She lived across town and no one knew where she lived. I left my kids with Deb until things cooled down back home.

Meantime, Deb said "Bob and CC's wife were still coming over looking for us". Onetime his wife even brought along her mother and they didn't want to leave; Deb ended up having to use physical force just to get them out of my apartment. # Get out!

However, one day Bob supposedly met CC's wife at my apartment and the two of them supposedly had a conversation. Bob later told me that "his wife tried to get him to sleep with her to make things even between us! However, he claimed that he didn't sleep with her but who really cared; I could have cared less!

Meantime, while we were still hiding out at Cindy's place somehow Deb forgot to mention that one day Walden stopped by! However, I didn't find this out until some years later; for some reason she didn't want me ever knowing that Walden came back; I always thought he just upped and abandon me for no reason!

After everything died down at my place CC and I went back home and all the drama was finally over; it was time for us to try and make that baby that I was so desperate to conceive!

Meanwhile, it was time to have my one day surgery since my period started back. I really needed to know if that meant that I could still get pregnant again! It was all I could think about; it was very important whether or not if I could still have any more kids!

However, after I had my one day surgery I could barely open up my eyes before the nurse said "I had to leave the hospital right away because they needed the bed space". I remember every time I tried standing up somehow I just kept falling back down!

I was so out of it but somehow I was finally able to get dress; but by the time I left that hospital I was still high off the anesthesia and it was still in my system in full effects; I was high as a kite!!

When I got home CC's step-brother stopped by with some cocaine called Ready Rock and asked if I wanted to try some. I didn't even know what ready rock was back then but since I was already still high off the anesthesia I said yes sure why not.

His step brother added the cocaine with a little baking soda and water onto a spoon; he held it underneath a lighter until it bubble into this little rock form shape; then he added it to some weed and we ended up smoking it inside of a pipe.

However, I was still very high off the hospital stuff so I really couldn't tell if that ready rock made me feel anymore higher; that was my first time ever smoking cocaine; I only snorted it before.

Meantime, I returned to the doctor for my follow up and he wanted to run another test on me. He took a small tissue sample from the lining of my womb and sent it to the lab to be analyzed.

When the results came back somehow it showed that the tissue samples came from the lining of a girl around nine years old. How was that even possible…? Was there a mix-up of some kind…? I was twenty-eight years old and not nine years old.

The doctor explained that after I had my baby and had to be given that D&C that somehow in the process of doing that it caused my lining of my womb to get totally scraped away".

However, due to me not having a lining was the reason why my periods stopped for those four years; those pains I felt each month was somehow from a new lining growing back inside me!

The doctors were truly amazed and stunned by all of this but I needed to know if I could still have more kid; unfortunately the doctor said "it would be very difficult to become pregnant again!"

The D&C caused a lot of scared tissues and I'd developed something called Endometriosis. However, the doctor didn't say it was impossible to get pregnant again; he only said it would be very difficult to conceive because of all the scared tissues I had.

At first, I was a little upset but I wasn't going to let what the doctor said discourage me from trying to make another baby; I kept my hopes high and had faith that one day it would happen!

Meanwhile, one day my oldest daughter came home from school with a bunch of scratches on her neck and said "her teacher grabbed her by the collar and scratched her neck up."

I believed my daughter was telling the truth because she wasn't the type of child that made things up. Also my next door neighbor's son said "he too witnessed unacceptable behavior".

I was so upset about the scratches being on her neck I went up to the school and confronted the teacher. Of course she wasn't going to admit to putting the scratches on her so I reported her to the Board of Education; however, they didn't do anything about it.

I then went to the police station and they said "unless my daughter had any broken bones or bruises on her body they couldn't do anything about the situation either"; # that sucked!

I was so mad that I ended up taking my daughter out of that school and put her into another school. I believed that the teacher lost her patience and really did grab my daughter by her collar.

However, I heard that shortly afterwards the teacher got fired for something else she'd did. See how things worked out; what goes around really did come back around. # God didn't like ugly!

Meantime, I started feeling really self-conscious about my weight especially since CC had all these muscles! Somehow I felt that I was too skinny for him; I only weighed a hundred and one pounds and I felt I needed to put some meat on my bones; you could see my ribs and I hated being that skinny all of my life!

I started taking these gain weight pills that the doctor gave me; however, that was a bad mistake! I went from wearing a size three and four to wearing a size fifteen in a short amount of time!

Later I ended up with a lot of cellulite all over my body; however, I remember a time when I didn't even know what cellulite was! Now I wish that I would have never taken those pills; that was so stupid of me and now I truly regret taking them!

Meantime, my job had their annual picnic and I decided to take CC to the picnic with me. When we walked over to where everyone was sitting the looks on their faces was priceless!

He wore shorts with a muscle shirt and all of my co-workers were staring at him; some of them were even going crazy over him. However, a co-workers that lived in the same building as CC's wife told everyone that "I was messing with a married man."

After she told them that everyone looked at me like I had two heads; the head housekeeper tried to get all up in my business and started asking me a million questions about him.

However, that was none of her damn business; stop being so damn nosey. So what if I chose to date a married man; that was my bad and I didn't have to answer to her or anyone else!

Somehow I was at the point where I didn't give a damn about what people thought about me anymore; they could think whatever they wanted to; somehow I just didn't care no more!

Meanwhile, I was twenty-nine years old... CC and I were still going strong; I was ready to settle down and try to have his baby!

At that time he wasn't working and my sister Bev helped him get a job at Swallens in their maintenance department. He met a guy named Jim-bow after he walked in on him smoking a joint in the men's restroom; after that they became life-long friends!

Meantime, my youngest daughter was in kindergarten and she gave me the scare of my life! It happened one day after I dropped her off at my friend's Sharon house so that she could walk to school with her daughter Lee-Lee.

Sharon lived right next door to their school but for some reason nobody knew that it wasn't no school that day. After I got back home Sharon called and informed me about the school being closed; she said her daughter came back without Monica; however, I didn't know where my child was! I was scared to death!

CC and I got into the car to go look for her; we looked down every street and all over the school grounds but didn't see her nowhere in sight; that day I ended up having a panic attack!

I was terrified thinking that something terrible had happened to her! I started praying really hard; I went back home in case somebody tried to call while CC continued to search for her.

When he returned home my daughter wasn't with him. I was just about to call the police when I got a phone call from a stranger saying that somehow "my daughter was with him."

At first I panic but then the man said that "he worked at a gas station down the street from my house and my daughter was there and she was safe". Apparently she stopped at the gas station to use their telephone on her way trying to walk home.

I was so relieved to see her when CC brought her back home; it's a good thing she knew her phone number. Thank God she was ok; good looking out to the man in the gas station!

Meanwhile, I needed to borrow some money from my dear friend Evelyn; I asked CC to take my car and go get the money for me. However, he picked up a friend on his way over to her house; somehow I wasn't even aware that he had picked up anybody.

He was gone for a long time and later Evelyn called and said CC never showed up; I started getting worried about him and wondered where he was and what was taking him so long...?

Later on that night a police officer knocked on my door and asked me my name and said that "my car was involved in some sort of incident that led CC into getting arrested". Say What...

I was freaking out and didn't know what was going on; the police officer said "they found stolen property in the trunk of my car and CC was taken to jail for receiving stolen property."

Apparently his friend had stolen something and placed it in the trunk of my car; somehow he left it in there after he got out. CC claimed he had no idea that his friend had stolen anything!

He ended up catching a case for giving his friend a ride and being in the wrong place at the wrong time. However, none of that would have happened if only he went straight over Evelyn's first.

He was taken to a jail called the work house and that next day I went to court to find out what was going to happen to him. However, due to his past record the judge set a really high bond.

However, I was shocked after hearing his rap sheet because of all the things that were listed on it. I remember sitting in that court thinking who the hell have I gotten myself involved with...? At first I thought I'd hooked up with a real criminal or somebody!

Later CC explained when he was in the Army he stayed in all kinds of trouble and that's why his rap-sheet was so long. I spoke to his mom after court to let her know what was going on with him.

I never met his mother before and this was my first time ever speaking with her. However, she didn't seem too interested in what I was saying; somehow she gave me the cold shoulder.

She did however say that "she wasn't putting up any bail money for him" and gave the phone to his uncle Harris. I then explained to him what was going on and he said that "he'd get back with me as soon as he consulted with a lawyer about it".

Meanwhile, I was lonely and upset; I started hanging with my sister's best friend Kim and we became close friends. However, CC was still sitting in jail while his so-called friend was free as a bird and still running around town doing whatever he pleased.

Meantime, his uncle said "the lawyer advised him that CC's friend not get caught yet; also to keep a very close eye on him so that he wouldn't try to run away and disappear nowhere".

He also said "even if CC didn't know that the stuff was stolen that his friend could still flip the script on him; he could be offered a plea bargain and somehow turn states evidence against CC"!

Meantime, his uncle Harris introduced me to CC's younger brother Willard; we kept in contact while CC was locked up. I started thinking that somehow CC was never getting out of jail.

I panic and ended up doing something that I shouldn't have done; I slept with Willard. I was lonely and I allowed myself to become very weak! Afterwards I realized that sleeping with him was a big mistake; I should have been much stronger than that.

Meantime, his uncle Harris said it was time to turn his friend into the police; however, I didn't ask no questions and I gave the cops the address to where his friend was staying at.

Meanwhile, a month had passed and CC was still sitting in jail. I couldn't take it no longer and I wanted him to come home. I would have done anything to help him get his freedom back!

I decided to call upon my ole friend Brother Me; he was crazy about me and would have done anything to help me out. I wanted him to bail CC out of jail. However, I knew it was going to be some kind of a catch and he was going to want sex in exchange for CC's freedom but that was a bullet that I had to bite!

I guess that's why I waited so long in the first place before asking for his help; I dreaded the consequences that I had to face! However, I had to do whatever it took in order to get CC out of jail. Even if that meant sleeping with Brother Me. # Oh well so be it.

CC had no idea what measures I'd gone through in order to gain his freedom back; in the long run it was well worth it. He was so happy to be out on bond and that's all that mattered to me!

On the day of his court hearing the judge dismissed all the charges against him; his case was thrown out of court. Hallelujah, free at last, free at last; thank God almighty CC was free at last.

Meanwhile, we tried building a better relationship and the sex between us was so amazing; I tried my best to get pregnant by him but it seemed like it was never going to happen!

Meantime, he wanted to get a divorce from his wife so that he could marry me! We went to the court house to inquire about getting a divorce without having a lawyer; he couldn't afford one!

The clerk was real helpful in assisting him; she showed him how to file his own paperwork through the court system; she also showed him examples of other people's divorce papers so that he could use them as a guideline when filing for his own divorce!

He took all the information that was provided to him and used it to work on filing for his divorce and then he took out the typewriter and started typing up his own divorce papers.

That next day we went back to the courthouse and filed his paper work with the clerk of courts; she said "based on his typing skills not to quit his day job because his typing was terrible".

They scheduled him a court date and on the day of his divorce hearing his wife showed up with some guy by her side! I guess he was supposed to be her real baby's daddy; CC wasn't.

Since there were no children or property involved in their marriage his divorce was finalized immediately. CC requested his X drop his last name & return back to her maiden name at once!

However, I ended up telling him about me sleeping with his brother Willard; I didn't want to start a marriage off by having any secrets between us! However, I did make one exception and I decided not to tell him anything about me and Brother Me!

At that time somehow it seemed like some secrets were better off left un-said; so I didn't say one word about me sleeping with Brother Me in exchange for him getting him out of jail.

Meanwhile, we ended up going to a justice of the peace and got married; my friend Evelyn and her boyfriend Harold came along with us as our two witnesses!

By the time I turned thirty years old...I'd been married for a month; however no one in my family believed that I was married. I even showed them my marriage license but somehow they still didn't believe me; they all thought that I was just making it all up!

Meantime, Vet got pregnant with her first child and she went into labor on Thanks Giving and named him Orlando. My nephew Doug also had a son named Arron by a girl named Sonya. Also my nephew Mookie had a baby girl by a girl named Emi.

It seemed like every time that someone close to me gave birth it was a quick reminder of the baby that I'd destroyed at age fifteen; this only made me want to get pregnant even more!

Meanwhile, I decided to quit my job at the Red Roof Inn; I wanted to devote all my time trying to get pregnant by my new husband. Getting pregnant again was all that was on my mind.

One day the head housekeeper pissed me off and I used that opportunity to walk off my job; I didn't tell anyone that I was quitting after working there for almost six years. Sorry Red Roof...

Meantime, CC's friend Jim-bow helped him get a job with some construction company; the job was only seasonal but it was better than having no job at all. Thanks Jim-bow!

———∞o◦❭◎❬◦o∞———

Meanwhile, I turned thirty-one years old…Somehow after seeing Tony that time at the Red Roof Inn the thought of trying to have another baby just wouldn't leave my mind for some reason!

My sister Vet ended up marrying her baby daddy Leo and for some strange reason he would always call me ghetto; however, I saw myself as being more like ghetto fabulous!

Leo was in the Navy and planned on going to Norfolk to check out where he was going to be stationed at. He and Vet needed a ride to Virginia and I wanted to ride along with them.

Somehow I knew my X David lived in Norfolk so I asked CC if we could take them there; I knew if he came along that I wouldn't be tempted in wanting to see David again.

However, I couldn't get in touch with CC the night that we'd planned on leaving; he was nowhere in sight and didn't appear to be going on the trip. I guess he really didn't want to go anyway; my friend Sharon ended up going on the trip with us instead.

I told Leo that he would have to drive my car since CC never showed up but somehow I knew that I was going to see David while we were there; I never had any closure with him either!

As soon as we arrived in Norfolk David was the first person that I called; I hadn't seen him since he first left to go in the Navy. However, he offered us to stay at his place instead of a hotel.

We all decided to take him up on his offer and stay at his place. I had no idea what he thought about me anymore and I didn't know if maybe time had brought back any unpleasant memories for him…?

I was hoping that he wasn't holding any animosity towards me for not knowing whether or not if Heather was his child…? Also the fact that I had Monica by his best friend Bob. However being in his presence I definitely felt some kind of regrets!

I overheard him talking on the phone to some girl; therefore I knew he had someone special in his life. However, the whole time I was there he made damn sure that we didn't bump heads!

Later that night Leo and Vet went to sleep in his guest room and David went to bed because he had to get up early for work; Sharon and I were in his living room watching TV and talking.

We were having a conversation about me not knowing whether or not if David or Lackey was Heather's father; however, after hearing Sharon's response somehow it totally shocked me!

She said "it was just something about David that made her feel that he was really my daughters true father and although she never met Lackey and knew nothing about him that somehow she still believe that for some reason David was her biological father"!

As we continued having our conversation for some strange reason I started getting really horny! However, I just knew if I got in that bed with David that I was going to do more than just sleep!

As the night went on all I could do was think about getting pregnant again! In the back of my messed up mind somehow it felt like David was the perfect candidate to get that job done!

I guess I thought if I got pregnant by him that somehow it would make things right between us again! However, I wasn't thinking clear and I forgot all about my husband back home!

Getting pregnant again meant more to me than anything in this world; even my own husband. I was horny as hell and on a mission to conceive another child no matter what the cost was!

After Sharon fell asleep I got into bed with David and I laid down next to him and tried to go to sleep. However, I was so wet down there that it felt like I had busted a nut on myself.

I went into the bathroom to check on myself and that's when I realized why I was so wet and horny! It was because my period came down. For some strange reason right before coming on I would always get really horny but I wasn't even due to come on!

However, that night somehow my own blood saved me from committing adultery; Lord knows if I hadn't come on I would have definitely had sex with David; I guess it just wasn't meant to be!

That following day he took us all out and wined and dined us; he also took me shopping for whatever I wanted. He showed us great hospitality and made sure that we all felt very welcome!

Meantime, Leo and Vet moved to Norfolk and David kept in touch with them. He did whatever he could to help out my sister and nephew and I appreciated him looking after them! Eventually somehow we lost contact and I didn't hear from him ever again!

Meanwhile, Vet moved back to Cincinnati and her husband was transferred to another base in Tennessee; Leo needed a ride to his new base so he asked CC if we could give him a ride there.

This time CC decided to go on the trip with us; my next door neighbor Cal found out about the trip and also wanted to go; he had relatives that lived in Memphis that he wanted to go see.

On our way headed to Tennessee Leo saw some of his Navy buddies on the highway; just as CC tried to catch up with them somehow the tire blew out and started shedding its rubber.

The car started swerving across the highway and we came really close to having a terrible accident. When CC pulled over to change the tire all the rubber had come completely off the tire!

After arriving in Memphis Cal took us to meet a few of his family members including his grandfather. Later he took us to another house that I thought belonged to one of his kinfolks; but it turned out that none of these people in the house were kin to him.

However, I had no idea that the house he'd taken us to sold drugs; I didn't find that out until we got on the inside and that's when I realized that Cal had taken us to a real live crack house!

All of the men inside were heavily armed with guns and I felt really bad that Vet was exposed to that type of atmosphere; she had never been in an environment like that before in her life!

I knew my baby sister was scared because that was my first time ever being in a house like that myself. I asked her and Leo to wait in the car while Cal, CC and I went into this empty dirty room that was supposed to be a kitchen but it didn't have any furniture.

In this room there were these guys getting high and they asked if we wanted to hit this pipe that they were smoking on. I thought they were smoking the same stuff that we called ready rock but whatever was in that pipe wasn't anything I ever had!

I only took one hit and it felt like I was about to have a heart attack; my heart started racing really, really fast and I needed to sit down quickly. I was about to sit on the dirty floor but instead I sat down on a dirty window seal. After that I was ready to get the hell up out of there and it was time to go; # let's bounce!

Everyone was very tired and since Leo didn't have to be back on base until that next morning we all decided to stay overnight. However, we tried to find a hotel but due to all the Navy guys in town everywhere was booked up. We couldn't find a vacancies nowhere in sight; everything was sold out for miles!

However, Cal planned on spending the night at one of his cousin's houses; she knew someone that owned some cabins in the woods that still had plenty of vacancies available.

His cousin said "since she knew the owners that we could stay there for free". Everyone was so exhausted and wanted to get some rest and going to the cabin sounded like a good idea.

However, it seemed like we were riding for hours out in the middle of Bum-Fucked Egypt somewhere. I remember thinking... what kind of backwoods does Cal's cousin have us staying at...?

When we first arrived I looked at the outside of these cabins and the first thing that came to my mind was the horror movie called "Motel Massacre". Cal dropped us off and said that he'd be back that next morning after he picked up another tire for our car.

I had a real bad feeling about being left out in the middle of nowhere; however, I thought that perhaps the inside of the cabin didn't look as bad as the outside did; the outside was horrifying.

Somehow I was wrong; the inside of the cabin was much worse than the outside was. When we first walked in I couldn't believe my eyes; it was downright filthy and disgusting and unreal.

I thought the crack house was bad but that cabin took the cake and words can't even describe how dirty and dreadful it was! It was no way I'd let a stray dog stay there less known a human!

Everyone was mad for being dropped off in that hell-hole! However, it was nothing that we could do about it; Cal was long gone and left us overnight in that disgusting place. # Lord help us!

However, we all tried to make the best out of a bad situation but that was highly impossible. It was no way that we were going to sit on those dirty beds; less known lay down and sleep on one!

The blankets looked like they hadn't been washed in over a hundred years and I bet the bed bugs were even scared to get in those beds because that's just how nasty and dirty they were!

However, I was too afraid to turn down the covers and look at the sheets because just looking at the blankets was enough for me! I think the ground outside looked cleaner then the carpet did!

The bath tub was so gross that it made us want to throw up and when we turned the water on it came out looking like mud. I thought the cob webs hanging in the windows were the curtains!

However, it was very hard to believe that the Board of Health hadn't shut that place down; it's a good thing that we didn't have to pay any money because somebody would have got their ass whipped. I thought I was dreaming or we was in the Twilight Zone!

CC and Leo ended up sitting on these two dirty chairs and Vet and I sat on top of their laps that entire night. Due to all the rodents and bugs running around made it impossible to get any sleep! When Cal came back to get us we all wanted to kill him!

Meanwhile, CC became best friends with a guy from our neighborhood that sold weed named Dudley. I started getting jealous of their friendship and wanted to do something about it.

CC, was always constantly hanging around him and smoking weed all of the time! It felt like my husband was more interested in Dudley's friendship than he was with trying to get me pregnant; so I decided to get close to him so I could destroy their friendship!

I knew Dudley could make babies because he recently got some girl pregnant. I figured I'd try to get pregnant by him and also ruin his friendship with CC and kill two birds with one stone!

However, conceiving another child was embedded so deep in my head that it was like a brain tumor growing inside of me! My biological clock was counting down and I was running out of time!

I cared more about becoming pregnant than I did about my own marriage! My husband cared more about smoking weed than he did about trying to get me pregnant; what kind of shit was that?

I eventually succeeded with my plan with Dudley and we started having sex behind CC's back; however, he had no idea what was going on and he continued being friends with Dudley!

However, that pissed me off to the point that it caused our marriage to take a wrong turn downhill; we started arguing all of the time and this caused CC to move out of the apartment; after he left I started letting Dudley spend the night with me sometimes!

Dudley was born under the Zodiac sign Leo and he had this way of getting under my skin! He knew how to push my buttons and I'll never forget when I let him use my car to take me to work.

That day we got into a big argument; however, it was so petty that I can't even remember what it was about but I do remember being so mad at him that I jumped out of my own car!

Meanwhile, I turned thirty-two years old… I was still messing around with Dudley and CC still wasn't back home yet.

Meantime, I developed a bad reputation in my neighborhood because people started catching on that I was having an affair behind my husband's back. Some of the females hated on me and some of the men also had some problems with me too!

One night, I went to this club where Deb worked at as a bartender and she hooked me up with free drinks all night long. I started thinking about what the doctors said about me trying to get pregnant and somehow this caused me to really start turning up!

That night I got so intoxicated that some females in the bathroom wanted to fight me! However, I was too drunk to even know what their beef was supposed to be about; I had no idea!

After the club let out Deb's boyfriend Lavey-boy drove us home; on the ride home he got really angry and started beating on the steering wheel; he started cussing and making all kinds of nasty remarks and saying all kinds of crazy and hurtful things.

I remember sitting in the back seat thinking why wasn't Deb saying anything to him and why was she just letting him go off on her like that; I was wondering why she wasn't speaking up for herself or saying anything to defend herself to him...?

Later that night I found out that he wasn't going off on Deb; somehow he was going off on me! However, I was so high that I didn't realize that I was the one he had the problem with! Oh well.

Meanwhile, my husband and I still hadn't got back together; I missed him and wanted him to come back home. Early one morning I decided to go look for him at his cousin's Roy's house. I was on this drunken rage and I woke up everybody in their house!

CC's aunt said that he wasn't there but I didn't believe her and busted in their house anyway! I started looking in closets and up under beds screaming for CC to come out. That next day after I sobered up I felt really bad because I'd made a fool out myself.

Meanwhile, there was a big drug bust where I lived. The D.E.A. and Swat team had the entire complex surrounded. Swat was hiding out in bushes and on top of the roofs looking for a neighbor that sold drugs; that day everyone in that neighbor's apartment went out in handcuffs; even the little kids! ☹!

Meantime, speaking of kids the girl that Dudley got pregnant had their baby. I was happy for him but at the same time I was also jealous; he had no idea how much I wanted to get pregnant.

However, one day I was joking around about kidnapping his baby and somehow he took me serious; I guess he thought I was like the lady from the movie "Fatal Attraction" because that's when things pretty much went downhill and eventually we ended things.

Meanwhile, I tracked down my husband and he came back home; we continued working on our marriage and I still wanted to get pregnant by him more than ever but I wasn't having no luck!

Meantime, I was on a waiting list waiting for these townhouses that went by your income. My sister's lifelong friend Trade-wind and I had been on that list waiting for a few years.

We applied for these townhouses long before CC and I ever hooked up. However, this move was going to be a fresh start for both my husband and I; at least at the time that's what I thought.

However, I didn't add CC to my lease when I first moved in; for one he didn't have no job or no income at that time. After I'd settled in I went to a doctor to see about getting some fertility pills!

However, I didn't have any medical insurance to cover the cost of the pills and they were very expensive so I couldn't afford to keep taking them; I eventually had to stop and that sadden me!

Meantime, the doctor suggested that CC get his sperm count checked to make sure that he wasn't having any problems; they took a sample of his sperm and send it to the lab to be analyzed.

I was willing to do whatever it took to become pregnant again; however, after CC's test results came back it wasn't good. The doctor asked if he smoked cigarettes and said that "smoking can have a lot to do with a man's sperm count being low."

I informed the doctor that CC was a real heavy weed smoker and smoked weed every day and that's when the doctor said "my husband's sperm count was so low that he couldn't get me pregnant standing on his head." # Yes CC was shooting blanks!

The doctor suggested that he stopped smoking weed for at least thirty days and eat certain types of foods to help build up his sperm count. He ate all of the foods but unfortunately he never stopped smoking the weed not even for one day; how very sad!

Never once did CC make that one sacrificed of giving up the weed in order to try and get me pregnant; however this affected me in a way that made me want to start cheating on him again!

Meanwhile, there was a young man named Darren that worked at my job at Children's Hospital; I started checking him out to become my new candidate for my potential sperm donor. However, because of my Endometriosis I knew I was going to need somebody young with some super sperm and full of babies!

Meantime, somehow my boss Cooper seemed to have no control over his employees and this made it really easy for me to have an affair right on my job; right up under my bosses nose!

The hospital owned a house down the street and Cooper assigned my co-worker Nelly and I to clean there three times a week. However, this was the perfect place to have sex at.

Darren always came to the house whenever I worked. Although he didn't have any kids I still felt that because he was so young that he could help improve my chances of conceiving.

I'll never forget the day that my boss almost walked in on us having sex; but thanks to my good friend and co-worker Nelly she was somehow able to prevent it from happening! Thanks Nelly!

Meantime, I wanted to get pregnant so bad that I improved my chances by adding some more sperm donors to my list; somehow I started back messing around with Dudley again.

I also added a guy named Dan to my list; he had a baby on the way so I knew he could make babies. However, everyone thought he was CC's little brother; they resembled one another.

I was really hoping that my husband would have just stepped up to the plate and stopped smoking the weed so he could have at least tried to get me pregnant himself but that was never going to happen! CC loved smoking weed way more than he loved me!

Meanwhile, by the time I turned thirty-three years old… I had stressed myself out trying to become pregnant again. I decided it was time to take a break and go on a family vacation for a while.

We planned a trip to Orlando Florida and my sister Vet, her son and my niece Robin also came along. I was so amazed when we first arrived; it was my first time seeing a palm tree in person.

We went to Daytona Beach to see the ocean for my first time and it was breath taking. I'll never forget seeing the sun rise coming up over the ocean; it was the most beautiful sight that I had ever seen.

I still didn't know how to swim but that didn't stop me from getting out there and enjoying all of Gods great water.

However, my youngest daughter and my nephew experience with the ocean wasn't so pleasant; they were in this floatation tube together and somehow a big wave came and swept them far out into the sea; I was so scared but thanks to CC's quick response somehow he was able to rescue them back to safety!

We loved Florida so much that we made a promise to go back every year but since we couldn't afford to take a vacation every year we went to all kinds of time share presentations just to get the free trips that they offered for attending their sales pitches.

Meanwhile, CC went on another trip by his self to Atlanta to see his family and he wanted me to come but at the time I didn't feel like going; getting pregnant was my # number one priority!

CC's cousin Rome and his brother Willard stopped by while he was away. I asked them to go get my friend Deb because I was boarded and needed someone other than them to talk to.

After Deb arrived we all sat around and listened to some music and chilled out. I started thinking about my medical situation; and just thinking about it made me so depressed.

Willard asked if I wanted him to call their mother and ask her why he and his brother didn't have any kids yet; he told me to be really quiet while I listened in on their phone conversation.

When he asked their mom why he and CC couldn't have any children somehow her response shocked me! She "said it was because of her magic moment." What magic moment...?

What the hell was that supposed to mean...? However, after hearing that unusual conversation somehow I was so confused and bewilder I ended up smoking some weed laced with cocaine!

Meantime, CC and I visited one of his aunt's and she told me something about his mother that threw me through a loop; she said "be very careful what I ate whenever I go over CC's mother's house because her sister knew Voodoo and to watch my back"!

Although I didn't fully understand what she meant by that I still took heed to what she was saying. I couldn't help but to wonder if that conversation between Willard and his mother had anything to do with his mother supposedly knowing Voodoo…?

Meanwhile, it was the Fourth of July and CC was supposed to take my girls to see the fireworks; instead he dropped them off at his mom's house and went somewhere with his brother Willard.

However, I was mad as hell when I found out that my girls were at his mother's house. Oh no he didn't leave my girls alone with that women. When they returned home I was so upset that I went completely ham on CC for leaving them with his mother.

All I could think about was everything that his aunt warned me about and the comment his mother made about her magic moments being the reason why CC couldn't have any children.

I told him not to ever take my daughters around that woman again and I called his mom a witch; however, he thought I called her a bitch and this led to our very first physical altercation!

We got into this big scuffle and I tried to kick him in his head but I ended up kicking the glass out on our headboard instead.

Meantime, we moved past our first big fight and I tried to put everything behind me and I still tried to get pregnant regardless!

Meanwhile, I turned thirty-four years old… Thanksgiving was coming up and CC's step-father and his mother invited us to Thanksgiving dinner. However, I tried not to think about what his aunt said and planned on going to their house for dinner anyway.

CC and I somehow decided to stop by their house the night before Thanksgiving; when we arrived his mom and step dad were in the kitchen preparing the food for that next day.

Somehow CC left me alone with them and I offered to help them in the kitchen. As I was helping them prepare the food out of nowhere CC's step dad asked me "if I believed in Voodoo"…?

As they waited for my answer all of the sudden they stopped whatever they were doing and both of them got very quiet and started staring at me and waiting for me to answer the question.

However, I wasn't the least bit shocked when he asked me that because of what CC's aunt had already told me; but it was still weird that he would just come right out and asked me that.

I answered by saying that "I wasn't saying whether or not if I believed in it or not but I did say that Voodoo wouldn't work on me because my mind was too strong for it to have any effects on me"!

After I made that comment they both looked at each other and didn't say another word and continued preparing the food. However, after that I really started watching my back; I knew there was a reason why he asked me that question in the first place!

Meanwhile, females where I lived tried to get me put out of my townhouse every chance they could; they would call the rent office and tell the manager all kinds of lies on me! I soon realized that I was living around a bunch of jealous bitches and haters!

Meantime, CC and I planned on attending my cousin Nee-Nee wedding in California. However, our transportation wasn't going to make it out there and it was no way I was going to fly.

We ended up getting roundtrip bus tickets and boarded the bus for a long three day ride out. However, that ride turned out to be one hell of an adventure; we met people from all walks of life!

When the bus made its first stop in Indiana there was this daring blind man that boarded the bus. He was traveling all by himself and I truly admired him for being so brave & courageous.

One night CC went into the restroom to smoke a joint and he opened up the window to let the smoke go out. Somehow the window was connected to the same window that I was sitting by and at that time the bus was going through a severe wind storm.

Somehow after he returned to his seat the window next to me suddenly flew open and the strong gust of wind almost caused me to fly out the window; it literally pulled me right out of my seat; somehow CC was able to pull me back down and held me tight!

It all happened so fast that I didn't know what was going on; the bus driver finally caught on to what was happening and he immediately stopped the bus and helped CC close the window!

However, during our bus layovers it was a big hassle trying to wash up in those public restrooms; sometimes the water was freezing cold and trying to sleep was crazy! Although I must say it was never a dull moment and something was always jumping off.

Somehow we ended up with a couple of crazy bus driver's and one of the drivers was making illegally pick up's! One night he picked up some random person from the side of the highway.

We were travelling down this dark isolated road and there wasn't any civilization for miles; the bus driver suddenly pulled the bus over and all of the sudden the windows started fogging up!

Then the driver announced that it would only take a few minutes for the windows to clear and once he gained visibility again that we'd be on our way; I believe the driver purposely fogged up those windows just so he had a reason to stop the bus.

While everyone sat there waiting patiently for the windows to clear out of nowhere some strange unknown person boarded the bus and suddenly the windows mysteriously started to clear fast.

That day the bus was full of passengers and the only seat available was the seat directly behind us; the one right next to the bathroom and that's where this strange person sat down at.

However, we couldn't tell if this person was male or female; it was wearing a red hoodie and had a very large head; perhaps it was an afro underneath the hoodie. I don't know; I couldn't tell.

This person was very dark complexion and their eyes were red as fire; everyone was trying to figure out what was going on and who was this unknown person that the driver had picked up.

However, after traveling for a while this person started making these really weird noises that sounded like some kind of chanting like sounds. By then I wasn't taking any chances; I didn't trust whoever this Devil looking person was that sat behind us!

From that point on it was no way that I was going to turn my back or go to sleep with this weird person sitting behind me; I wasn't letting this spooky looking person stab me in my back!

I started peeking through the cracks of my seat and keeping a close eye on this person the entire bus ride. I stayed up all night making sure that this person didn't try nothing stupid or crazy!

When the bus arrived at its next scheduled stop the driver told the stranger to get off the bus! However, this person refused to get off so the bus driver ended up using physical force on him!

I guess whatever money that little red riding hood paid under the table must have ran out and that was the end of the line for this person and I was so relieved that I could finally relax again!

In the meantime there was another bus driver that left people whenever we stopped for layovers; if anyone wasn't back when they were told to be the driver left them. Some people got left at a restaurant out in the middle of nowhere; I made damn sure that we were always back on time; I didn't want to get left behind.

We had another bus driver that held everyone hostage; one of the passenger's bus ticket was stolen from their bag and the driver refused to drive anywhere until the missing ticket appeared.

The bus driver held up the bus for hours before going to its next destination; I don't know if the stolen ticket was ever recovered or not; I do know it put the bus way behind schedule!

All in all the bus ride to California was one exciting ride of a lifetime and my cousin's wedding was well worth that long ride out and we had a wonderful time; I will never forget going on that trip!

Meantime, I turned thirty-five years old... I still hadn't given up on becoming pregnant. We kept our promise and took our yearly vacation to Florida; we visited Orlando's Ripley's Believe It or Not; I rubbed their fertility statue but it didn't do me any good!

Meanwhile, my ex-boss Cooper got another job supervising downtown at the AT&T and Hilton hotel building and he offered me another job cleaning on both sides of that building.

Shortly after I got hired somehow he lost his job and he was replaced by another man who became my new boss. I met two co-workers named Belinda and Jan and we became good friends.

One day Belinda and I were having a conversation about my mother forcing me to kill Tony's baby and that's when she told me that "he was somehow related to her"; # it's a small world after all.

Belinda and I worked on the weekends without having any supervision; we pretty much were able to do whatever we wanted to; somehow my mission to get pregnant was still on the horizon!

I started messing around with one of the guards named Zack; at first it started out as just a mind game but somehow it got out of control and he became another one of my sperm donors!

I met people from all walks of life while working on the hotel side. One night I wasn't feeling well and I met this professional basketball player; however, he thought because he was famous that I should have been jumping through hoops over him!

I guess he thought that I was some sort of groupie or something...? He got a serious attitude because I didn't know who he was! He said "everybody knew him!" However I didn't care who he was or how famous he was; to me he was just another guy I didn't feel like being bothered with at that particular time!

Meantime, the hotel side hosted their annual Christmas in July event; every year they held big parties for all the gay people and the trans- genders and swingers from all over the world.

These festivities lasted three days of celebration; the first night was for the gay men and the second night was for the gay females; the third night was for the swingers and trans-genders.

I'll never forget the night the gay females all got together; it was hard to tell some of them apart from the real men; however some of those females looked just like straight up dudes.

One of my co-workers name Charley yelled out to the single females "Fresh meat available." Then he pointed to me and Belinda; however, that caused mass females to come after us!

However, I don't have anything against gay people; I say to each his own; whatever floats someone's boat as long as they're happy it doesn't matter what sex a person loves; just as long as they love! However, that night Belinda and I had to play like we were a couple just to keep some of those women up off of us!

Meantime, something was always happening on the hotel side; it was never a dull moment. One night this fat drunk guy checked in; he asked Belinda and me to get him a luggage rack.

We thought it was so strange that he asked us for a cart and didn't have any luggage; however, we got him one anyway and that's when he started pulling out these big stacks of money!

That's when we realized that this guy wasn't fat; he was just loaded down with lots of money! He pulled money from out of his coat pockets, his pants pockets and even out of his socks and shoes; # money was stashed everywhere on his entire body!

After he finished stacking all of that money onto the cart somehow it filled the entire bottom; he asked us to hold open the elevator doors while he pulled the cart inside. Right before the doors closed he reached down and handed us a stack of money!

Meanwhile, I got laid off from my job and CC wasn't working either! I applied for welfare assistance before my unemployment kicked in. This was the time the haters where I lived really tried to get me put out of my townhouses for some reason or another.

There were so many jealous women that hated on Trade-wind and I that it became a total nightmare! It got so bad that we couldn't even bring home any shopping bags or they'd call the rent office and the welfare and make up all kinds of things on us!

I received a couple of unemployment checks but somehow before I had the chance to report them to the welfare the haters had already had them investigating me for some unknown reason!

However, this caused me to catch a case with the welfare; they said I didn't report my income and I owed them some money; however my sister paid them back but somehow I still ended up with a record and later I was able to get those charges expunged.

The situation kept getting worse where I lived and I only dealt with Trade-wind and my other three neighbors, Michelle Carla and Lou. The rest of them bitches I didn't fuck with or trust!

Meanwhile, Kurt Russel and Sylvester Stallone were filming a movie in Ohio and CC auditioned for a part as an extra in the movie called "Lock up"; somehow he was able to get the part.

Meantime, we took our yearly family vacation to Florida but this time we took along three of my daughter's closes friends; Piggy, Keshia and Monique came along on the trip with us.

However, by me coming from a family of all girls CC wasn't too happy being surrounded by a bunch of females; somehow he seemed to always be in the company of the ladies; six on that trip!

---oo◦)◉(◦oo---

Meanwhile, by the time I reached thirty-six and thirty-seven years old... I started losing a lot of my loved ones; my aunt Achkels that communicated with the dead spirits passed away.

Also my life-long friend Ronnie who I grew up with also passed and my sister's Tonya and Lisa's grandmother passed. Shortly afterwards Ronnie's father also passed away along with my grandfather Dave. God bless them; may they all rest in peace!

However, before my grandfather passed he was in the hospital on life-support and the hospital wanted the family to make a decision whether or not to leave him on it.

All of my sisters got together to discuss what should be done; I told them to leave me out of it. I wanted nothing to do with deciding someone else's faith; I just couldn't bear to be a part of that kind of decision; I wasn't playing God with anybody's life!

However, after my grandfather passed I made up my mind that I wasn't looking at anymore dead bodies ever again! I had seen enough; I was done looking at anyone else lying in a coffin!

Meantime, after going through all those deaths finally it came some life; my niece Erica gave birth to my great-nephew Darius. Soon afterwards my sister Vet gave birth to her second child Alexis. Once again everyone was having babies but me...

---oo◦)◉(◦oo---

Meanwhile, by the time I turned thirty-eight years old... Vet married another man named Vernon. Their wedding took place on a river boat and their daughter Alexis was going to be their flower girl and I was responsible for getting her to their wedding.

Somehow on the way there we started having car trouble and they were already married by the time we got there; Alexis missed their wedding and couldn't be their flower girl. Sorry!

Meantime, I got a job working at a nursing home and the girl that lived across from me also started working there. During this time Trade-wind and I had already figured out who the main person was calling the welfare and rent office telling on people.

I tried to warn the girl not to trust her neighbor because the main snitch lived right next door to her; the reason why I warned her was only because we worked at the same job together.

I wasn't trying to be friends with this girl; I just didn't want her running her mouth and telling her business. I knew that the snitch would get her into serious trouble for not reporting her income!

Sometimes, I would see her having long conversations with the snitch and that really bothered me! I wanted her to know who not to trust and who the real enemy was that lived amongst us!

However, somehow this girl thought that I was the snitch and she continued being friends with the enemy; she didn't want to trust me and this resulted in her doing jail time. I tried to warn her but she just wouldn't listen! Oh well; I guess she knows now...?

Meanwhile, somehow Trade-wind got a job working in the rent office; she no longer had to worry about the snitches or the haters calling the office and telling anything on her anymore!

I however was still a target for the haters to mess with! It was only a matter of time before one of them called the rent office making up stuff and trying to get me in trouble and put out again!

Meantime, sure enough the rent office started getting calls reporting CC living with me! Sure I could have just went ahead and added him to my lease; he had no job or income no way!

However, I felt like why should I; almost every women that lived up there had their baby daddies and husbands living with them; none of them were on their leases! Trust me; they weren't.

Somehow it didn't even seem to matter no more; I'd had enough and wanted out of that place! My oldest daughter was about to graduate and I planned on moving out right afterwards.

In the meantime, my father was under the care of his ex-wife and somehow his health took a wrong turn for the worse; he ended up in a nursing home and I was highly upset about it.

I wanted him to come and live with me whenever I moved; however, he ended up passing away before that could ever happen! God bless his soul and may he also rest in peace!

However, my father's obituary contained information about all of my sisters and maybe somehow Trade-wind must have left his obituary lying out in the rent office somewhere...?

Because somehow the manager saw it and realized that CC was using one of my sister's address as being his place of resident. However, the manager had the nerve to go over my sister's house to question her whether or not if CC lived there! Please tell me since when do rent managers go outside their properties to question other people...? Where they do that at ...?

Anyhow, my sister wasn't available for any questions so the manager said "they were going to do a full blown investigation on me." I told her that I was moving out right after my daughter graduated and she agreed that I could stay there until then.

---000-)◦(-000---

Meanwhile, I turned thirty-nine years old...My time on becoming pregnant was running out but I still refused to give up trying!

Meantime, one of my daughter's classmate's father was looking for someone to clean an office building where he worked; he set up a meeting to discuss getting the cleaning contract there.

I'd signed a written agreement with the rent office saying that I would move right after my daughter's graduation; however, if I didn't move they were going to pursue the investigation on me!

I hurried up and packed all of my things; I was ready to get away from all the haters, backstabbers and snitches. I wanted to move away and live my life in peace and harmony for a change!

CC, and I wanted to move in a new home but we knew that we couldn't afford one so we tried to buy a brand new three bedroom mobile home. We were afraid that our loan wouldn't get financed because we previously filed for a chapter-7 bankruptcy.

CC's work history put us in a bad financial situation and we ended up turning all of our debt over to this credit counseling establishment. However, they weren't doing their job properly and somehow it left us with no other choice but to file for a bankruptcy.

Meantime, somehow our loan was approved and we found a nice mobile home park for our brand new home to sit on; we also ended up getting that cleaning contract; this was a huge blessing!

However, my youngest daughter was going through her teenage rebellious stage; she didn't want to move out of the townhouse because she didn't want to leave her friends behind.

I still had a couple of weeks before I had to move so I let my girls stay at the townhouse while CC and I moved into our new mobile home; I couldn't wait to get away from that dreadful place!

Meantime, my niece Robin gave birth to my great-nephew Vernon and I still wanted to conceive a child more than ever and I sure as hell wasn't giving up on trying to become pregnant.

However, CC still wouldn't stop smoking the weed long enough to build up his sperm count; this only made me want to look for another potential candidate to become my sperm donor!

Meantime, my youngest didn't like her new school; it was a predominantly white school and somehow she couldn't seem to adjust. She asked to drop out and go to Job Corp; I signed all the necessary paperwork and she attended the one in Dayton Ohio.

—∞o⟩●⟨o∞—

Meanwhile, by the time I turned forty and forty-one years old... I was still determined to have another baby; however, I figured since my mother and oldest sister had their babies late in life that maybe somehow it meant that I too still stood a chance!

Meantime, my friend Brother Me passed away; he often told me stories about him serving in the Vietnam War and being sprayed with some kind of chemical called "Asian Orange".

He said "being exposed to that chemical would eventually turn into a rare form of cancer and slowly kill him over the years." I guess it finally caught up with him...? May he also rest in peace!

Meanwhile, by the time I turned forty-two & forty-three years old... Death came and took away more of my loved ones...

My sister Lisa's husband George passed away and not long after his passing; she and Tonya's dad also passed away. I also lost two of my closes friends; Pamela Jean and Lena both passed away. May God bless their souls and may they all rest in peace!

Meantime, there were a lot of unexplained things happening around the house that we couldn't figure out why or how they were happening; all kinds of crazy things were going on.

One day my oldest daughter had all these bruises all over her body; however when we questioned her about them she had no idea how they got there! At first we thought maybe someone might have beaten her up and she was just too afraid to tell us!

Meantime, someone told us that they actually saw her laying on the floor having a seizure; however, this was my very first time discovering that she was really having some full blown seizures!

When she was almost seven her teacher mentioned something about her having twilight seizures; however, back then I never witnessed any of them! I didn't become fully aware of her having any seizures until she turned twenty-two years old. This explains all those unexplained things that happened in our house!

I truly believe her seizures resulted from when I was pregnant with her and the doctor put me on those birth control pills; her seizure seemed to be hormonal. Every time she had one they seemed to always be around the time of her menstrual cycle!

Meantime, my niece Tamara had her first child; my great niece Na'zaine was born. Once again someone in the family had another baby! I was very happy for her but very sad for myself.

Meanwhile, when I turned forty-four years old...One of CC friends worked for the same company we had our cleaning contract; CC hired his friends son name Lil' Marvin to work for us.

When Lil' Marvin first started working for us I didn't think too much about him; other than the fact that something about him reminded me so much of a young Tony when Tony was fifteen.

Somehow Lil' Marvin's great resemblance of him made me want to get pregnant even more then I already did; I guess because somehow he brought back past memories of the baby that I'd destroyed when I was fifteen. Somehow it felt like all those memories came rushing back to bite me on my ass once again!

Lil' Marvin was a nice looking young man with a head full of hair; he had a beautiful smile with a nice chocolate complexion; he was only nineteen years old but somehow I thought he was much older; I guess because of the way he carried himself.

However, after him working for us for only a few weeks I started looking at him in a whole different kind of way! I saw him as becoming my future baby daddy; it became quite clear that I had to have him and somehow he was going to get me pregnant.

The cougar inside of me emerged and I had to have sex with him A.S.A.P! Every morning I got the chance to see and talk to him and somehow he gave me this great big boost of energy!

It was so weird how much he resembled Tony and sometimes I couldn't take my eyes off of him! However, looking at him was also a painful reminded of my mother forcing me to kill Tony's baby and this caused some bittersweet moments at times! He was born under the zodiac sign "Virgo" the same sign that Walden and Lackey was; who would have ever thought that...?

Sometimes I'd stare at him so hard it made my husband start to get suspicious of me and one time CC even said that "I look at him as if he was some kind of teen idol or something."

However, that didn't stop me from checking him out; I was on a serious mission to get his sperm inside of me and I was determine one way or another to become pregnant by him!

In the meantime, I found out that he had a girlfriend and a daughter; I was happy to know that he could produce children. However, I wasn't concerned about him having a girlfriend; it was no way that I was going to let her stop me from getting with him!

As time passed my husband suspicions grew even stronger! My flirtatious ways became so obvious to everyone around me! Everyone knew how bad I wanted that young man; however, everybody but him because for some reason he was still clueless!

In the meantime after Pamela Jean passing somehow I felt it was my obligation to look after her one and only son Jamie; we let him stay with us and gave him a job working the third shift.

Every morning when picking up my daughter and Jamie from work I was able to be in Lil' Marvin's presence. However, CC ended up stopping him from sitting around and kicking it with us; he made damn sure that we kept it moving so that I wouldn't be able to be around him anymore; I was highly pissed off about it.

However, after my husband stopped me from seeing him I felt so dead inside! Soon my time was running out and my biological clock was going to stop ticking forever; all the odds were stacked against me! This was the point come hell or high water I was determined to somehow find a way to get pregnant!

One morning while CC was still sound asleep I decided not to wake him and went and picked up my daughter and Jamie by myself. I wanted to see Lil' Marvin to let him know how I felt about him; this was the perfect opportunity to make my move on him!

When I arrived at the job site I asked him to ride with me to drop off Jamie and my daughter; I dropped them off down the street from my house; I didn't want to take any chances on CC waking up and busting me with Lil' Marvin in the van with me!

I drove to a nearby park that was close to the job and found a secluded spot to park. I had a little weed and asked him if he wanted to smoke a joint with me! Right after I finished rolling it a police officer came out of nowhere and walked towards the van.

However, somehow I was able to throw the joint down before the cop saw it. He knocked on the window and asked if everything was ok and said that "he saw the van parked back in the corner and just wanted to make sure that everything was alright".

I told the officer that we were on our lunch break and everything was just fine and he left. However, I wasn't going to let that cop stop me from getting Lil' Marvin's sperm inside of me!

I let out the bed in the back of the van and asked him to join me. After smoking the joint I tried to explain to him how much I really needed to have sex with him. Somehow in the process of trying to explain my feelings suddenly I just jumped on top of him!

I started seducing him into having sex with me and he was so shocked; he didn't even know what hit him! No way did he see that coming! I'd jumped his bones so fast before he even had the chance to realize what was happening to him and it went down!

However, that was just a quick previews of what I had in store for him. I think by him knowing that I was married to the boss it somehow must have frightened him a little; # you think...?

Sexual harassment wasn't even the word for what I did to him; it was more like taking full advantage of him! Desperate times called for desperate measures and I was desperate as hell.

Meantime, we started getting a lot of complaints about his job performance; they weren't satisfied with his work! CC decided to take him off the first shift and put him on second to help keep down the complaints; he had no idea that I had slept with him!

I started going to the job site and checking on Lil' Marvin; I could tell that he was still a little afraid of me; I felt kind of bad about taking advantage of him so I started adding a little extra cash onto his paychecks each week; hoping that might help ease his fears! I didn't want him being afraid of me in any kind of way!

Whenever he came to pick up his paychecks his girlfriend and daughter would always come with him. I'd always dot the "I" on his checks with a heart instead of just putting a dot.

One day his baby momma saw the heart on his paycheck and she got very upset; she became suspicious of me and started questioning him about my intentions. Shortly after that it seemed like it was almost impossible to ever have sex with him again!

Meanwhile, the complaints continued about the quality of his work and CC was ready to fire him but still not knowing we had sex! I talked him into putting him on third shift; it was less work.

Meantime, CC started cleaning another building and this made it easy for me to see him without CC being around; one night I went to the job site and tried to get together with him again!

We left the job site and I offered to take him out to dinner; he didn't want anything to eat so we took a ride instead. I found a secluded spot to park the van and once again I let out the bed.

However, this time there were no surprises; he knew exactly what to expect. I even heard him mumble under his breath "if it wasn't for his baby momma he wouldn't have no problems being with me"; unfortunately that night I still didn't get pregnant!! # ☹!

Meantime, somehow CC found out that I was giving him extra money on his paychecks but the job was still complaining about his work performance; this made CC wonder why I was giving him extra cash when he wasn't doing a good job!

We got into a big argument over the money and in the midst of our heated conversation somehow I just blurted out that I had sex with Lil' Marvin and what the hell did I do that for...?

Eventually CC ended up firing him due to his lack of work and I felt really bad about how everything turned out; perhaps if I'd never told CC anything about us having sex then maybe I could have convinced him to transfer him to another building.

I wish I'd never opened up my big mouth; I became so depressed that I shut down! CC ended up calling a couple of my sisters and nieces over and they tried to give me an intervention about my major obsession for Lil' Marvin; however, it didn't work!

Meanwhile, it felt like I was dying inside and I truly needed something to make me feel alive again! However, the only thing that was going to pull me out of my depression other than getting pregnant was finding the opposite sex to play mind games with!

I started playing them with this guy that also worked at the same building we cleaned. I wasn't attractive to him but he was the perfect guy to play mind games with; he had a weak mind and I definitely was going to use him for it; # let the games begin!

This guy believed anything I said and did whatever I told him! One time, he came over and cooked a five course meal for me and my husband; he also brought other gifts to the job as well.

However, I knew I was misleading him by letting him flirt with me! He really thought he stood a chance; he thought he was one step closer to having sex with me but little did he know that it was never going to happen! Eventually the mind game ended in a major conflict between him and my husband! # Game over!

Meanwhile, my niece Marla called upon CC and I to help her out of a situation that she had gotten herself involved in; it was dealing with her boyfriend drama; somehow she needed our help!

However, this situation put us in the middle of what could have been a fatal tragedy! I felt that because she put us in that kind of dangerous situation that she owed me big time! # Pay up!

Meantime, Lil' Marvin hated my guts; however I was still determined to win him back regardless. I saved up enough money so I could give him at least one month's salary; I felt really horrible about how things turned out between us! I wanted it to be right again; hopefully by giving him some money might help a little!

I put the cash inside of a card and gave it to Cindy's niece named Jean; she lived in the same housing complex he lived in and she planned on giving him the card whenever she saw him!

However, I didn't mention to her that I'd put any money inside the card. On the night that she gave it to him she said "he immediately threw it in the dumpster without hesitation". He didn't even bother opening up the envelope to see what was inside of it!

Later that night I went through hell looking in that dumpster for that envelope! However, with a little luck somehow I was able to find it amongst all that trash! Thank Goodness for that!

A few days passed and I still couldn't wrap my head around how much Lil' Marvin hated me! I wanted to do something about it so one day I tracked down Cindy at her doctor's office. I needed her to take me to his house so I could give him the money myself.

After I gave him the money he seemed to be very grateful to get it. However I could tell he felt kind of bad once he'd realized that he had thrown away the card that had the cash inside of it!

I felt a little better after giving him the money but I just knew I'd probably would never be able to have sex with him ever again; however, I refused to go down without a fight; let round one begin!

Meanwhile, I started doing all kinds of crazy stuff; I mailed all kinds of cards to his house every day, two and three times a day; trying to make him understand that I wasn't giving up on him!

I even went as far as involving his father by also giving him a letter trying to explain to him how much I really needed his son involved in my life! I was just a total mess point blank period!

I was so desperate to be with that young man that I started drinking and getting high every day! I started riding around his neighborhood and stalking him! Somehow I became this out of control obsessed ticking time bomb that was ready to explode!

One night in the wee-hours of the morning Jamie and I had been drinking and we both were drunk. Somehow we ended up riding past Lil' Marvin's house! However, there were a bunch of guys standing in the middle of the street in front of his house.

I didn't expect to see anyone out that time of morning but somehow Lil' Marvin was standing outside. However, I panic and stopped dead in my tracks! I didn't want to drive pass him but I had no other choice; everyone had already spotted my big van.

I put the petal to the metal and went flying down the street like a bat out of hell; everyone scattered like roaches to get out my way; I was driving like I was on the International Speedway!

Meantime, my bizarre behavior and my quest to conceive a child by him didn't stop; nor didn't I stop talking about getting with him. Things around my house became really bad and somehow I just couldn't let go of the fact of trying to get pregnant by him!

CC and I were constantly always arguing over my insane need to be with Lil' Marvin; his name became like some kind of product in my household! This situation caused a huge problem and it took a toll on everybody around me including my daughter.

One day she was working at that same building his father worked at and there was some conflict between them. I guess because of all the confusion that was going on in my house must have somehow caused her to take her anxiety out on his father.

Somehow my daughter lost it and she ended up hitting his father in the head with a mop after he walked on her wet floor. The fact of the matter was my wanting to conceive a child by Lil' Marvin caused everybody around me to just go completely crazy!

Meanwhile, my daughter wasn't the only one that flipped out so did my husband. It was one day CC lost control and snapped out on a friend of my daughter's named Keshia.

Keshia also worked for us at the same building as Lil' Marvin father; sometimes she would see him whenever he came to pick up his father from work and she would always give me the 411.

She would also give me a full report whenever she saw him. One day she was telling me something about Lil' Marvin and I guess CC must have somehow overheard our conversation.

He got so upset he took his anger out on her and went too far overboard; they got into a physical altercation and somehow he ended up pushing her so hard that she flew across the room!

However, I felt really bad because her mother and I were good friends and I didn't want any animosity between us! # Sorry!

Meanwhile, when I reached the ages between forty-five through forty-seven years old... I still wasn't letting go of trying to become pregnant again!

My niece Robin gave birth to her second child; my great nephew Maleak was born. Once again someone else in the family had another baby but it still wasn't me; why can't it be me...?

Meanwhile after the 911 tragedy we lost one of our cleaning contracts. Losing it put us in a bad financial situation because we still had all of the same bills but not the same money anymore!

Meantime, I met one of CC's friends named Dale; at first I didn't know that he was related to Lil' Marvin but I found out that they were cousins. However, after meeting him somehow it gave me hope again on carrying out my plans to still get pregnant.

Somehow I got access to Dale's phone number and I started calling him and asking him questions about his younger cousin; somehow he gave me Lil' Marvin's cell phone number and I started texting him but he didn't know that it was me texting him.

Dale had no idea what my real purpose was or why I was so interested in his younger cousin but somehow he seemed to be willing to go along with the program! I asked him to come over so that I could discuss the reason why I really wanted his cousin.

However, I could tell that he was nervous about coming because he didn't know what to expect. Although he and CC were pretty good friends that still didn't seemed to help matters any!

Somehow by him helping me with his cousin made him very paranoid; he had no clue where my husband fitted in all of this; by him knowing that CC was going to be home I guess he probably thought I'd invited him into some kind of lion's den or something.

However, he still showed up but he brought along his posse; at least five or six other guys showed up with him but CC knew all of them. I had been drinking and smoking weed long before they got there so therefore I was already toasted when they arrived.

I guess Dale brought along his posse just in case my husband tried to get stupid with him or flip the script on him because that night he had no idea what was going to jump off!

However, CC and the other guys stayed in the kitchen kicking it and getting high while Dale and I sat in the living room discussing my situation about his younger cousin.

He was a big help in keeping me connected to his cousin but one day he told me he was moving to Atlanta. He was my only hope of getting close to Lil' Marvin and I didn't want him to go!

I found it to be quite coincidental that Dale was the exact same age as my oldest daughter and his cousin Lil' Marvin was the exact same age as my youngest daughter; # How ironic!

He and I became good friends and I was very sad after he moved away. However, we continued to keep in touch with one another and he was just a phone call away! Whenever I felt sad or depressed somehow he always seemed to make me feel better!

One day while taking our yearly trip to Florida we stopped outside of Atlanta at a random gas station to get gas. Somehow out of nowhere we saw Dale. It was so good running into him out of the blue like that and it was also a very strange coincidence!

However, I took seeing him again as being some sort of sign and it was definitely meant for me to see him again. He'd suggested that we stopped by and check out where he was living and CC and I stopped by his house before heading to Florida.

After that day our friendship grew even stronger and he and I could talk about anything and everything; we helped each another by coming up with solutions to help solve one another problems!

I remember one time being really depressed and I started crying over the phone; Dale knew how upset I was and offered to come back to Ohio just so he could hook me up with his cousin!

I couldn't believe that he got on an airplane and came all the way back to Cincinnati just to help me out; I admired him for being such a good friend and I deeply valued the friendship we shared.

When he arrived in Ohio he booked a motel room and had me wait there until he went to get his cousin. When they returned he left so that I could spend time alone with Lil' Marvin.

I could tell that Lil' Marvin was nervous because I was just as nervous as he was; it was our first time seeing each other in a long while. We smoked a couple of joints and I got the chance to have a nice conversation with him; he wasn't mad at me anymore!

We started off by kissing and having foreplay! However, right before we were about to have sex somehow he had a premature ejaculation! I guess he was so nervous or excited that somehow he busted a nut before he even got the chance to put it inside me!

I felt something wet running down my legs and after that he couldn't get another erection although he kept trying and trying! After a while of him continuously trying to get it up I just said don't even worry about it and suggested we try again some other time!

Sure, I was disappointed but things were still good between us; that was all that mattered to me at that moment. However, I was looking forward to getting together with him in the near future!

Lil' Marvin called Dale to come and get him and we made plans to see each other again to finish what we had started. Little did I know then that it was never ever going to happen again!

I headed over my friend's Cindy house after I left the motel and Dale called and asked me how things went between me and his cousin; he wanted to know if everything was ok and if I wanted him to come back to the motel so that we could talk about things.

I guess Lil' Marvin must have told him about what happened or shall I say what didn't happen. However, if I'd went back to that motel that night Dale and I would have done more than just talk.

Although he had no interest in me what so ever I still didn't trust myself being alone with him. I was in a weak and fragile state of mind and after what just happened with his cousin who knows what I would have did with Dale...? # It aint no telling!

Meanwhile, my niece Marla told me information about Lil' Marvin that really shocked me; she told me that they had been working on the same job together for quite sometimes but for some reason she waited a long time before telling me this!

Somehow she discovered that he was the same guy that I'd been obsessing over and she was also one of the family members that came over and tried to give me that intervention!

Marla and Lil' Marvin had discussed all kinds of things about me long before she decided to tell me anything; that's probably why he and I never hooked up again like we'd planned on doing.

However, I serious felt that blood should have been thicker than water and with Marla's help I could have had the perfect opportunity to get closer to Lil' Marvin; however, I think she was looking out for her Uncle CC and not her blood Aunt O'Gram!

Marla said "she didn't want any parts in my scheming to get closer to Lil' Marvin" but if that was the case then why did she get all up in my business and go behind my back and let him know that she was related to me...? I felt if she didn't want to get involved then she didn't have to tell him anything about me at all.

Especially that we were kin to each other; however, I felt when she first found out who he really was she should have just kept it to herself and kept her damn mouth shut! As long as she waited to tell me anything she might as well not even told me nothing at all. A lot of good it did me; it did me no good at all.

Meantime, I became so angry and upset with my niece that I stopped talking to her. I felt like she was ruining my life because Lil' Marvin was my last and only resort of getting pregnant again!

However, I felt in my heart that she still owed me big time for the time that I got involved in her boyfriend drama; the drama that almost caused CC and I to get killed. But that's ok; it's all good.

Meanwhile, Dale moved back to Ohio and I was so happy to have him back in the same town again! Somehow he gave me this great sense of hope on trying to still get pregnant again!

I told him all about the situation with his cousin and my niece and how she was conflicting against me; he said that "he would get to the bottom of things and find out what was really going on"!

Later Dale came back and said "whatever my niece told his cousin it caused him to never want anything else to do with me ever again". Say what; what the hell...?

At that point I really started hating Marla guts; I even stopped going to all the family functions because I just didn't want to be in the same room with her anymore or be anywhere near her again!

I became so depressed that I slowly started dying inside; my need to conceive was at its wits end; getting back with Lil' Marvin was over said and done with! Somehow my own niece took me back to ground zero! Stick a fork in it because it's a done deal!

Meantime, I was in a very dark place always crying and thinking about my time to conceive was over. One day Dale stopped by and saw how unhappy and depressed I was.

He started saying all kinds of good things to me; however, I didn't know whether or not if he was just saying them to make me feel better or what…? But hearing him say the things he said somehow made me feel this great sense of comfort again!

Meanwhile, there were no signs of Lil' Marvin ever coming back into my life again but his cousin was still there one hundred percent. Somehow, I started having these thoughts about Dale and I couldn't help but to feel a certain type of way about him!

However, he did have a certain swag about himself and my feelings for him started to change; somehow I'd developed these overwhelming feeling for him and his D.N.A started looking just as good as his cousin's D.N.A; Lord help me; # here I go again!

Meantime, I wanted Dale to know how I felt but I was too scared to tell him. I didn't want to ruin a perfect friendship so I'd beat around the bush whenever I talked to him. I just didn't want to come right out and tell him that I was starting to feel for him!

However, I felt he was also beating around the bush always trying to get me to say whatever it was before he responded back. Somehow I got the impression that we both were on the same page but neither one of us wanted to be the first to cross the line!

The situation between us reminded me of the record "Lovers & Friends" by Usher, Little John and Luda Chris. It was as if we were singing that song to each other; those words fit us perfectly.

Meanwhile, we became friends with benefits and somehow we crossed that line and our friendship was deeply compromised. We were at the point of no return and there was no turning back; we already had sex and the damage was already done!

However, the only thing that he really wanted was just an oral transaction. Somehow I knew his cousin probably already bragged about how good it was! It seemed like he couldn't wait until I did him too! Giving him oral sex couldn't have gotten me pregnant; now could it! Not in this lifetime; not by a long shot.

Dale felt that my vagina should have been for my husband only and off limits to everyone else! True that! He was so right but CC just wouldn't fully commit to trying to get me pregnant.

Regardless of what CC's mother said about her magic moments being the reason why he couldn't have any kids; he still could have at least did what the doctor asked him to do!

Stop smoking that Kush for at least 30 days; if only he just would had made that one little sacrifice for me but unfortunately he never did; # not even for one second less known thirty days!

However, when I first got married I never planned on being some kind of unfaithful adulteress T.H.O.T; but somehow my obsessive need to conceive again turned my life in that direction!

Perhaps if I had money I could have sought professional help and freeze some of my eggs but I didn't have any money so I had to go about it the old fashion way! That was to have sex and hope and pray that in the long run that I'd somehow get pregnant.

Meantime, one night Dale and his son went to the Drive-Inn movies with us and my niece Na'zaine also went. Dale sat up front with CC while I sat in the back with the kids.

As we sat there watching the movie I leaned over the back seat and somehow I must have accidentally touched Dale's shoulders. However, it wasn't in any kind of inappropriate way; it was very innocence but I guess CC must have saw me touch him!

On our way home I noticed that my husband wasn't saying anything; he was quiet and acting very cold towards me! I could tell he had some sort of attitude but at the time I didn't know why.

When we got home CC said "he saw me touching all over Dale at the Drive Inn". I was so speechless because I couldn't believe he said that; I could see if I'd touched him in a sexual way!

However, I reinsure him that there was nothing going on between us and somehow I was able to convince him that I had no interest in Dale what so ever. From that point on I had to be careful with my feelings and not let them become transparent.

I didn't want my husband ever knowing that I was messing around with Dale; him knowing would only add more salt to his wounds; he still wasn't over the fact that I'd slept with Lil' Marvin!

Meanwhile, I continued having an affair with him behind CC's back in hopes of becoming pregnant again but we kept it on the down low! I didn't dare want to jeopardize his friendship with CC in any kind of way; he trusted Dale and they got along great and he even let him spend the night at our house a few times!

However, this arrangement allowed me to continue to carry out my affair right under my husband nose; it was so easy for me to have sex with Dale without even leaving home! Shame on me!

I knew it was wrong and downright cold-blooded but then again desperate times called for desperate measures and boy was I desperate to have another baby in my life! What can I say!

Meanwhile, Dale drove our van to Atlanta and somehow while he was there he got involved with some female! However, he didn't want to come back to Ohio when he was supposed to.

This was the point when our friendship started spiraling downhill; he tried to play me like a sucker! I should have known once I smashed my homey that our friendship was never going to be the same and somehow a great friendship was totally ruined.

Since he refused to bring the van back when he was supposed to I told him that I was going to call the police and report it stolen; I also spoke to the girl that he was involved with and I ended up having a few unpleasant words with her as well.

However, Dale got mad at me for talking to his girl and he tried to throw me under the bus! He was going to text CC and tell him everything about our affair. However, at that time I had CC's cellphone and I was able to intercept his text. I responded back by making him think that CC had already knew all about our affair!

Since he thought that CC already knew he didn't bother going any further texting anymore details. I stopped him before he'd text something that he'd later regret; # nipped that in the bud.

Meanwhile, one night CC went out with his friends and my baby daddy Bob called; he wanted to come over and see his daughter but she wasn't at my house but he still wanted to come and see my other daughter. However, I didn't see any harm in him coming so I told him that it would be ok for him to come over.

However, he didn't feel comfortable being at my house; he feared that CC would get upset if he knew that he was there; he suggested getting a hotel room for my daughter and I to hang out.

Somehow after only being in his presence for just a short time a strange feeling came over me! I felt like something bad was about to happen! I was ready to go back home because I just kept getting this feeling that something was terribly wrong!

Bob had been drinking and was in no condition to drive us back home right then so I called our daughter and she came and got us. I saw our truck in the driveway so I knew CC was at home.

As we approached the house we heard this loud beeping noise but we couldn't figure out where it was coming from; the closer we got to the house was the louder the noise became!

When I opened up my back door somehow a big puff of smoke hit us in the face. My cat ran outside and started gasping for air. Oh my God is my house on fire; what is going on...?

After I got inside I saw all this white smoke and I covered my face and started opening up all the windows; I was still trying to figure out what was on fire! I yelled for CC but he didn't answer.

Once I went into the kitchen that's when I realized that the smoke was coming from the stove; CC left something in the oven and it was burnt to a crisp and somehow the pan was on fire!

I opened up the bedroom door and CC was lying in the bed passed out with the ceiling fan running; however, he was so high and intoxicated that he didn't even hear the loud smoke alarm going off; luckily the smoke hadn't reached the bed room yet.

However, if we didn't get home when we did it could have been a tragedy! My husband and cats would have probably died from all that smoke and our mobile home would have been toast.

That night I just thank God for giving me that uneasy feeling that made me want to get home; I made it there just in time to save my husband, my cats and our mobile home! Thank God!

So if you ever get the feeling that something wrong please take heed and don't hesitate! Always listen to your gut feelings because it could save your life or the life of someone else!

Meanwhile, Dale still hadn't brought our van back; he was too busy sucking up under his little girlfriend. I guess he thought I was playing when I told him that I would call the cops on him.

However, I wasn't playing and I did end up calling the police! They called Dale in Georgia and told him that "if he didn't bring the van back ASAP it could result in him being charged with grand auto theft". Dale forced my hand and left me no other choice!

However, he claimed that the van was broken down and that's the reason why he hadn't come back home but somehow after he spoke to the police he hurried up and came back to Ohio!

To be perfectly honest I really didn't want the van back! I just wanted him to come back home! After he returned we somehow continued our affair and picked up where we left off at.

Meanwhile, I turned forty-eight years old...and I knew it was highly impossible to get pregnant again but I still wasn't giving up!

Marla gave birth to my niece Bri; however, I was still holding a grudge against her for how she played me concerning Lil' Marvin; this caused me not to bond with my great niece! Sorry Bri.

However, right before I turned fifty years old...somehow I finally decided to end my four year old grudge that I held against her; I had already missed out on so much of my niece's lives!

Meanwhile, I turned fifty-one years old... This was the point when destiny was going to let history repeat itself again and I was about to get a huge wakeup call along with a very rude awaking.

One day my niece told me that someone named Walden called my sister's house looking for me and he left his phone number for me to return his phone call as soon as possible.

However, after hearing that he was trying to contact me after twenty-three years this left me speechless and lost for words. I didn't know what he could have possibly wanted with me!

However, it's funny how things turned out and how some things are just meant to be! Destiny had a strange way of showing up when I least suspect it to. Just think if I'd never ended that grudge with Marla then she would have never told me he called.

Walden was involved in some kind of accident in Wisconsin and the cops found a gun and marijuana in his possession; he was facing jail time and he wanted to see me before his hearing.

I was under the impression that he was no longer married anymore but I was wrong; he was still married but he wasn't involved in the church anymore; somehow he got kicked out.

For some strange reason I had no memories of him other than the ones when we were fifteen; somehow all those memories of the last time I saw him at age twenty-eight were totally gone!

After he refreshed my memory it all came rushing back like a light bulb went off inside my head and suddenly I remembered everything! Like the song by Keyshia Cole called "I Remember".

However, Walden was much more than just being my first or my X; he was like the reincarnation of his cousin Connie; I think the day that he found her lying dead in her bed was the day that her spirit somehow continued to live through him!

For that reason alone and no matter what I will probably always have some sort of a connection with him that will keep us friends for a very long time to come!

In the meantime one day he asked me to go for a ride; I had no idea where he was taking me but somehow we ended up at his house. His wife was at work and he wanted me to come inside!

I really didn't want to go inside but somehow he talked me into going in. However that's when I found out that he was a bigger weed head than my own husband was. # Puff, puff, Pass!

Although, I'd quit smoking weed he talked me into smoking a joint with him. Not only did I smoke weed with him I somehow ended up having sex with him in the bed he shared with his wife!

OMG...Here I go again! However the thoughts of me still trying to get pregnant was still in the back of my mind even at the age of fifty-one; I wasn't giving up until I had my very last period!!!

Meanwhile, Walden's court date was coming up and I prayed that he wouldn't get locked up; I was very concerned about the outcome of his trial and I wanted to be there to give him support.

I asked my husband if we could take him to Wisconsin to his court hearing and he said "yes"; however, CC had no idea that I had slept with Walden and believe me I wanted it to stay that way!

On the day of his trial I just kept praying that everything would work out ok. I didn't want to lose him after just getting him back into my life again. God must have heard my prayers because the judge let him go with only having to pay court cost.

On our way home from Wisconsin Walden and I fell asleep and somehow CC got lost and we ended up in Chicago. Since everyone was so tired Walden suggested we get a hotel room.

We got one room with two beds; CC was really exhausted so he fell fast asleep! Walden and I decided to leave out of the room and we decided to go for a walk and check out the town.

Somehow we ended up having sex in the men's restroom of the hotel lobby; my hormones were crazy and somehow in the process of having sex I ended up coming on my period. When we returned to the room CC was wide awoke and pissed off at me!

Meanwhile, Walden and I became totally out of control and somehow we manage to make up for all the lost times that was wrongfully taken away from us by Lackey at the age of fifteen.

We had sex everywhere imaginable; we even went as far as having sex in the cemetery where Connie was buried. Our sexual desire became so outrageous that if left us with little or no respect for our spouses. Somehow we didn't care that our behavior was hurting them and we continued our affair right in front of their face!

However, when Walden and I married our spouses it was for better or for worse! Well it definitely couldn't have gotten anymore worse than it already was! Somehow in the back of my sick mind I started thinking maybe he was back in my life to get me pregnant.

My actions became so out of control I went as far as going over his house even when his wife was at home; she wasn't going to stop me from getting with him; somehow I didn't care anymore!

However, his wife ended up hating CC, even more then she hated me! I guess the reason why she hated him so much was because he couldn't stop what was happening; somehow CC ended up hating her too; they became # number one enemies!

I even took out a restraining order against her just in case she tried coming after me! Somehow I was in complete control over Walden's mind, body and soul and it wasn't a damn thing that she could have done to stop me; I had his nose wide opened.

Our need to be together and my deep obsession to conceive another child was really reckless and I do deeply apologize to both my husband and his wife for our hurtful behavior. Sorry!

Not to make any excuses but it was a long overdue matter that lived deep inside both of us for many years; somehow this was a necessary evil that needed to get out of both our systems!

In the meantime I tried reaching out to Walden's mother; I wanted her to pray for me for the way that I carried on with her son but somehow I think she felt I wasn't worthy of her prayers!

I also wanted to clear up a rumor that I heard a long time ago about her supposedly thinking that "I had something to do with Connie's death"! I needed to get to the bottom of that rumor because I would have never did anything to ever hurt my best friend in any kind of way! However, his mom denied the rumors!

Meantime, I became so confused about the real purpose why God brought Walden back into my life again; somehow I knew the reason definitely couldn't be to get me pregnant.

However, I truly felt in my heart that the reason was something much more powerful than us just living out our teenage years that was wrongfully taken from us but what was it...?

I'm a strong believer that things just don't happen for no reason and there's always a reason behind each and everything that we encounter in our lives! However all the dots hadn't quite connected and I couldn't figure it out until one day it finally hit me!

It was the day Walden and I had a conversation and somehow the subject came up about my mother forcing me to self-abort my un-born baby when I was fifteen years old.

He wanted to know if there was any way possible that the baby I was forced to get rid of could have been his! However, after he asked me that somehow it really did something to me!

Somehow it opened up the gates of hell and all those old memories of me killing Tony's unborn child came rushing back like a never ending story; once again I was flooded with regrets!

However, after discussing the matter with him it was No way that the baby could have been his! I got pregnant long after we broke up and since I didn't have sex with Lackey it came down to only one other person that was the father of that unborn child.

The only other person that I had sex with at age fifteen other than Walden was my second love; my high school sweetheart Tony and it was so crystal clear without a shadow of a doubt whose baby my mother forced me to kill back then; I knew for a fact that it was JP's X boyfriend Tony that had got me pregnant!

In the meantime Walden reminded me of how much I loved journalism and writing; he suggested that I write a book and share my life story with the world and bring closure to the baby that I was once forced to get rid of. I definitely needed closure on that.

I said sure why not what do I have to loose...? Although I hadn't wrote anything of any real significant since high school I told him I'll write a book and I'll even go one step further and write it independently without seeking any professional help! However, I do plead the 5th on any and all mistakes found in this book and I do apologize for each and every one of them!!! "Sorry"!!!!!!

However, that was it that was the real purpose why Walden was back in my life again; somehow God made him a messenger to enlighten me on doing what was intended all along; to write about the horrible thing that my mother forced me to do! Maybe writing about this could set me free and finally bring some closure!

Maybe then what happened won't be in vain anymore! However, if that wasn't enough to convince me that writing a book was my real purpose then what happened next surely did...

It was one day after getting my yearly mammogram and I was told that they detected something in my left breast; they wanted me to set up an appointment to come in and get a biopsy!

The night before my biopsy I had this dream that warned me about having some sort of short lived health problem. However, ever since my near death and outer-body experience somehow my dreams always manage to reveal any hidden truth within me!

On the day of the biopsy they took several tissue samples to be analyzed; during the biopsy they placed a clip inside my breast to mark the location of the area that the samples were taken from.

However, before the lab results came back I left everything up to God. Somehow when the results came back in it did show that I DID have breast cancer... OMG what am I going to do!!!!!!!!

There I was done wasted almost a whole life-time trying to get pregnant and then to find out that I had breast cancer! This was a rude awaking and somehow it made me look at life in a whole different kind of way; it made me realize just how precious life really is and what's really important to us on this earth!

Meantime, I needed to have surgery so I met with a surgeon to set a date for my operation. The day before my surgery Walden treated CC and I to dinner and guess who we ran into..? It was Lil' Marvin's cousin's Dale; he was sitting in Olive Garden with his future wife to be; at first I didn't even recognize him. How ironic.

However, on the day of my surgery both CC and Walden came with me to the hospital; I said "the more the merrier"; I needed all the support that I could get during my time of crisis!

The receptionist at the hospital said "I had the same exact birthdate as her and she also said my name sounded like a famous person's name". However, I guess anything's possible! Maybe somehow by me writing this book will bring me my 15 minutes of fame...? Who knows...? Will just have to wait and see!

After I got settled in the hospital somehow Walden had the entire hospital staff tripping off of me; he told everyone that I was married to both him and CC at the same time! He had all of them thinking that I was some kind of bigamist or something. However, it was so embarrassing having everybody thinking that about me!

However, there was a problem with the clip that was placed inside my left breast; at some point and time apparently it moved out of place! Right before the surgery they placed a wire inside my breast so that the surgeon would know exactly where to cut.

Meantime, my surgery went off without a hitch and my recovery also went well. When I returned for my follow up the surgeon told me some unexpected news that really shocked me!

He said "All of the tissues that he removed showed No signs of cancer and they were perfectly good healthy tissues". Say what...? Can you repeat that again please; # I didn't understand!

I was so confused but then the surgeon went on to say that "during the time they gathered all those tissue samples during the biopsy that it's possible that the biopsy itself could have taken out all of the cancerous tissues that were inside of my breast"!

However, they still wanted me to have sixteen treatments of radiation following my surgery. Wait a minute now...I started thinking long and hard. If all of the tissues that the surgeon cut out of me were healthy tissues and showed no signs of cancer then why do I still need to have the sixteen treatments of radiation...?

Then I started thinking maybe since the clip had moved out of place that somehow maybe the wire was placed in the wrong spot and maybe the surgeon cut me in the wrong spot due to this!

I was so confused and I didn't know what to think. I thought maybe some cancer was still left inside of me somehow! I couldn't wrap my head around what was happening!

The surgeon explained that the radiation was just a precaution for any remaining tissues that surrounded the affected area; that it would help keep the cancer from least likely to occur!

However, since there was NO signs of any cancer found during my operation; I felt that the surgeon had already cut out enough tissues surrounding the area that he was talking about.

Bottom line I ended up refusing the sixteen treatments of radiation. However, since I refused the radiation the doctors wanted me to take some pills as another precaution!

When I looked up the side effects of those pills it wasn't good. They were supposed to help keep the cancer from coming back in my breast but at the same time it could also possibly cause cancer in my uterus; and to me that made no sense!

So bottom line I also refused to take the pills! I just decided to leave everything up to God and prayed that my surgery would be enough! So far so good at least that's what I thought right then.

However, when I went to have another mammogram the doctors thought they saw something else in my breasts and this time they wanted me to have another biopsy on both breast.

While giving me the biopsy the doctor had to suddenly leave out of the room without finishing numbing both of my breast. Therefore this caused me to go through the remaining of the biopsy without having any numbing medicine in one of my breast and this was very painful; somehow I managed to get through it.

When the doctor stuck me with that needle trying to numb me somehow the numbing medication accidently got squirted into her eye and as a precaution for her she ordered me an Aids test!

I'd just went off my period prior to having that biopsy but somehow the biopsy brought my period right back on; however that was the last period that I ever had! # No more periods!

However, I did say once I had my last period that I would give up trying to get pregnant again! It was finally time to give up after spending almost a whole lifetime of trying. # I surrendered!

However, I'm pleased to say that both the biopsy and the Aids test both came back negative. Hallelujah, I was free from having any cancer and I didn't have Aids! Thank God All Mighty!

Meantime, after going through my breast cancer episode I developed some kind of nervous condition that causes me to somehow pick on myself. When I get real stressed I pick my cuticle around my finger-nails until I make them bleed; I also do the same thing when plucking out my eye-brows hairs; sometimes I break the skin so I can get to the hairs that are underneath!

However, by me doing this it somehow seems to calm me down. I remember it was a time I couldn't understand how people could just cut themselves but now that I've developed a similar habit myself I understand why people do such disturbing things!

Meanwhile, I saw something on television that literally blew my mind. It was the day that Simon Cowell first announced who his judges were going to be on his new television show called "The X-Factor". This was when I first saw the man whose baby my mother forced me to kill and I couldn't believe my eyes!!!

This was the icing on the cake and somehow I knew right then that it was definitely a sign for me to tell my story to the world. Seeing Tony again made me realize exactly what I had to do and it was no doubt about it; it had to be done! So be it...

Somehow I may have wasted an entire lifetime trying to get back a baby that I was never going to get back but I guess it was God's plan along for me to live out my life so that I could write about it. However, this just goes to show that God really does..... Work in a Mysterious Way!!

However, I do Thank God for blessing me with the two beautiful daughters that he'd given unto me! However, due to circumstances beyond my control unfortunately I was never blessed with any grandchildren! However I have learned to accept my fate and I finally understand; if it's not meant to be it won't be!

Now that I've shared a fraction of my life story with you. You can judge me if you want to but at the end of each and every day...It won't matter because ONLY GOD can Judge me now!!!

☺ LOL☺ *Shade Free Zone* Revelation 20: 12-13 ********
THE END.................. to hopefully a new beginning..........